PUSH OPEN THE WINDO\

CONTEMPORARY POETRY FROM CHINA

Push Open the Window

Qingping Wang
Editor

Sylvia Li-chun Lin
Howard Goldblatt
Translation Co-editors

Copper Canyon Press
Port Townsend, Washington

Copper Canyon Press is in residence at Fort Worden State Park in Port Townsend, Washington, under the auspices of Centrum. Centrum is a gathering place for artists and creative thinkers from around the world, students of all ages and backgrounds, and audiences seeking extraordinary cultural enrichment.

This anthology is part of an international literary exchange between the National Endowment for the Arts (United States of America) and the General Administration of Press and Publication (People's Republic of China).

ART WORKS.
arts.gov

LIBRARY OF CONGRESS CATALOGING-IN-PUBLICATION DATA

Push open the window: contemporary poetry from China /
Qingping Wang, editor; Sylvia Li-chun Lin and Howard Goldblatt, translation co-editors.

   p. cm.

Includes bibliographical references.

ISBN 978-1-55659-330-7 (alk. paper)

1. Chinese poetry—Translations in English. I. Wang, Qingping. II. Lin, Sylvia Li-chun. III. Goldblatt, Howard

PL2658.E3.P87 2011

895.1'15208—dc22

2011015941

98765432 FIRST PRINTING

COPPER CANYON PRESS
Post Office Box 271
Port Townsend, Washington 98368
www.coppercanyonpress.org

ACKNOWLEDGMENTS

The title of the anthology is derived from a line in Qing Ping's "A Poem Written on an Overcast Day."

Shelley Wing Chan's translation of Qin Xiaoyu's "Tailing Dam of Baotou Steel" first appeared in *Virginia Quarterly Review*, Fall 2010.

The following poems first appeared in the online journal *Free Verse*, Winter 2010: Yibing Huang and Jonathan Stalling's translation of Mang Ke's "Sunflower in the Sun"; Joseph R. Allen and Ji Hao's translation of Shu Ting's "Higher Duty"; Tze-lan D. Sang's translation of Wang Xiaoni's "Betrayed by a Piece of Cloth"; Richard King's translation of Gu Cheng's "Birthday"; Haowen Ge's translation of Zhang Shuguang's "What Can I Say?"; John Balcom's translation of Wang Jiaxin's "Pastoral Poem"; Christopher Lupke's translation of Xiao Kaiyu's "North Station"; Nick Kaldis's translation of Zhang Zao's "A Year of Letters"; Kuo-ch'ing Tu and Robert Backus's translations of Cai Tianxin's "Variations on a Winter's Day" and Hu Xudong's "A Man Reciting Aloud on the Beach"; Gerald Maa's translation of Hai Zi's "A Poem Dedicated to the Dark Night"; Michael Gibbs Hill's translation of Ye Hui's "Inheritance"; Diana Shi and George O'Connell's translation of Shu Cai's "Tranquility"; Michelle Yeh's translation of Xi Du's "Poem of Death"; Steve Riep's translations of Zhou Zan's "Wings" and Duo Yu's "Village History"; John A. Crespi's translation of Yan Wo's "To My Husband, Mai Xiaoke, in 2007"; Paul Manfredi's translation of Ma Hua's "Crossing Baimang Snow Mountain"; Heather Inwood's translation of Leng Shuang's "Comb-Shaped Bridge"; Shelley Wing Chan's translation of Qin Xiaoyu's "Badanjilin Desert."

Jonathan Stalling's translation of Shi Zhi's "This Is Beijing at 4:08" and John Balcom's translation of Bai Hua's "Summer Is Still Very Far Away" first appeared in *Great River Review*, Spring/Summer 2011.

Christopher Lupke's translations of Sun Wenbo's "On Climbing Shouxiang Mountain Number 2" and "On Climbing Shouxiang Mountain Number 3 (after a visit from Liu Zongxuan and Ah Xi)," John Balcom's translation of Wang Jiaxin's "Drinking with His Son," Lucas Klein's translation of Qing Ping's "Confucius," and Alice Xin Liu's translation of Sen Zi's "Burning Leaves" first appeared in *Five Points* 14.1 (2011).

The board and staff of Copper Canyon Press wish to express their utmost gratitude to Alison Lockhart, whose tireless dedication to the press's mission and values has deeply benefitted this volume.

CONTENTS

EDITOR'S INTRODUCTION

Qingping Wang, *translated by Gerald Maa*

It is safe to say that Chinese achievements in written verse over the past two decades have been ignored. In a fairly large context—even global, if I can be forgiven a slight exaggeration—most literary critics and significant numbers of readers prefer to discuss or have only heard about China's narrative prose. In some countries Chinese poetry is synonymous with Tang poetry and Song lyrics. Especially troubling is the fact that a lack of familiarity with and understanding of recent Chinese poetry, especially that which has appeared over the past twenty years, exists among readers in China as well. Given the country's vast population, the sheer number of poets, poetry readers, and critics is substantial. Regrettably, most people have little or no appreciation of the best of today's Chinese poets and their work. Much of the poetry collected in this volume will, at the very least, reveal to the readers of poetry in two countries—the America of Whitman, Stevens, and Frost; and the China of Qu Yuan, Du Fu, and Ai Qing—the true features of China's fine contemporary verse. One may even hope that these readers will find the selections refreshing and eminently worthy of critical discussion.

For a variety of well-known reasons, contemporary Chinese poetry languished for a very long time; most of the poems that appeared during this period lacked basic poetic qualities. After 1976, Chinese poetry began a gradual transformation, achieving a degree of normality by the late 1980s. However, prior to 1990, the poetry scene was, to a certain degree, constricted by factors having nothing to do with poetry. Many poets (including a small number who would later gain well-deserved recognition) lost focus in the face of broad-based social activism and cultural radicalism, which adversely affected their ability to write. In 1990, a few ambitious poets began to distance themselves from the clamor of culture and society, immersing themselves in meditation on and the discovery of poetry itself. They spent an enormous amount of time involved in a comprehensive program of reading the best poetry available in China and devoted themselves to the acquisition of an understanding of the personal creativity and unique craftsmanship inherent in canonical poets, foreign and domestic, of each historical period. They overcame the urgent desire to write more and more attention-getting poems. With little or no fanfare, they effectively fostered a well-balanced poetic sensibility. In time more and more poets with a sense of poetic mission joined their ranks. Then, in the mid-1990s, these poets produced the first batch of outstanding work; in the two decades since, even more poets have created fine examples of modern verse, until there is little difference in quality between the best of today's Chinese poetry and the best of contemporary world poetry. In fact, a few Chinese poets have produced work in recent years that has elevated them to the front ranks of world poetry. Regrettably, too many people in the poetic realm—including readers, poets, and critics—are still confined to backward concepts, indulging in the habitually lazy poetic ideals of twenty years ago and even earlier. It is reasonable to imagine that a meticulous analysis and assessment of contemporary Chinese poetry remains difficult and exhausting, owing to a number of complex factors.

Although the finest work has appeared in the twenty years since 1990, "contemporary Chinese poetry" has had a timely entrance in literary history. From a historical perspective, the "great" of "great poets" and "great work" is relative in terms of time and place. The selection of poets for this volume includes a balanced representation of age, location, school or faction, and style. Admittedly, even a "balanced selection" cannot be completely divorced from the bias and limitations of the person doing the selecting. As editor, I wish to point out that while the current state of Chinese poetics may not exist in this book with absolute precision, I can say without fear of contradiction that most of the selected poets and their work, whether viewed in relative or absolute terms, represent the very best that China has to offer.

TRANSLATION CO-EDITORS' PREFACE

Sylvia Li-chun Lin and Howard Goldblatt

When we agreed to take on this exciting project as translation editors, we were reminded of a comment that has long resonated with us, as readers and translators of Chinese literature and as "shameless" promoters of the best of it, in the original when possible and in translation otherwise. John Cayley, himself a translator and a publisher of Chinese poetry in translation, has written: "Incontestably, the translation of classical Chinese poetry into English has given us a body of work which is culturally distinct from the poetry of its host language but which has immediate appeal, and is often read with intense pleasure and a deep awareness of its moral and artistic significance." The challenge, for us, was to assist in bringing over *contemporary* poetry from China such that Cayley's assertion could be modified by replacing a single word and remain true.

It would be difficult these days, given the quantity of translated poetry available from cultures all around the world, for anyone to accept Robert Frost's definition of poetry as "what is lost in translation." We prefer Eliot Weinberger's dictum, "Poetry is that which is worth translating. The poem dies when it has no place to go." When dealing with languages as different as Chinese and English, the search for equivalent expressions, for corresponding terms and forms, in translating verse requires not only linguistic sophistication but also profound cultural understanding and a creative streak. Is translating poetry difficult? Of course. Does it differ from translating other literary genres? Yes. Can it be faithful (whatever that ultimately means)? Without question, when it is done well.

Presented with a corpus of poems in Chinese by fifty poets writing over the past three decades, we were given the task, and afforded the distinct pleasure, of accomplishing three separate but linked goals: First, and least enjoyably, space limitations made it necessary to trim the Beijing editor's total (150 poems) down to a number that, when doubled (by the original texts) did not exceed our mandated length; that meant the loss of some very good poetry. Next, we scoured four continents to find the best Chinese-English translators available—our invitation was fervently accepted by nearly all we contacted—men and women whose exceptional work graces the pages that follow. Faced with the diverse backgrounds, poetic sensibilities, and personal styles of the poets, we assigned translators to no more than three poets—and in most cases, only one. That worked to create individualistic voices on the page. Finally, and most pleasurably, we worked with the translators to tease out as much as possible what was intrinsic to, and often hidden in, the works. The compact, highly allusive, and often abstract nature of poetry in general, and Chinese poetry in particular, led to sometimes widely different interpretations; the ensuing give-and-take—sometimes heated, but seldom contentious—both underscored the ambiguity of the original text and provided often inspired solutions. We believe that the dialogue worked to produce translations that will stand the tests of time and analysis. The fact that this is a bilingual volume informed our suggestions in some cases, but where differences of opinion existed, the translator had the last word.

The arrangement is chronological, for that offers the added feature of demonstrating how Chinese poetry has evolved over the quarter century, and a bit more, since the end of the Cultural Revolution. A few of the poets included here have died, several of them, perhaps surprisingly, by their own hand; all but one or two of the living poets reside in the People's Republic and subsist (it is as hard to make a living as a poet in China as it is elsewhere) in such disparate fields as teaching, editing, publishing, science, business, and government. A few graciously made themselves available to their translators for consultation, something that is almost always beneficial to the finished product. Biographical sketches for the poets—as well as for the translators—are included here.

Among the more than forty translators, who live and work in the US, Canada, China, Hong Kong, and Australia, are academics, graduate students, freelance translators, writers, editors, even a poet or two. Most worked alone, while for some it was a collaborative venture. Their professionalism, their respect for deadlines, their gracious acceptance of suggestions—often nothing more than calling attention to other possible interpretations—and their dogged determination in making cases for their choices were exceptional. Readers who know both Chinese and English are encouraged to look at both versions—while such readers might intuitively start with the Chinese original, doing it the other way round works just as well—to get an idea of the difficulties the translators faced and the superb way they overcame them. By any standard, each version is capable of, to repeat John Cayley's contention, providing "intense pleasure and a deep awareness of its moral and artistic significance."

In addition to the translators and, in some cases, the poets themselves, we have been aided in our work by the attentive encouragement of the National Endowment for the Arts, the originator of this anthology and its companion volume (American poetry into Chinese). Our publishers, Michael Wiegers and Alison Lockhart of Copper Canyon Press, gently kept us on message and deadline, set and frequently allowed us to alter parameters. Our heartfelt thanks to all.

Note: Often the poets dated their work (a more common practice in Chinese poetry than in the West), and we have retained these dates in the English translations.

OPEN WIDE

Forrest Gander

What comes to be remembered of an era of unprecedented development and technological progress in China, a time of brilliant architectural achievements, rapid advances in medicine, and the spread of literacy?

If the era we're talking about is the Tang dynasty, when Chang'an became the biggest city in the world, when the longest canal on earth was imagined and constructed, and when China asserted itself as a world power, many of us might say that what we remember best is the poetry.

Contemporary China, experiencing a new period of astonishing development, may leave a comparable legacy. The last thirty years, in particular, witnessed a flourishing of Chinese literature. Language is always the sharpest witness to change. So the poet Sun Wenbo claims we "must always / Look to language to be our witness."

Push Open the Window quickly gets going with Shi Zhi's bitterly sarcastic counsel that we "please firmly believe in the future / Believe in the never-ending struggle." So, at the start of these pages, the old language, its slogans and platitudes, is plowed under, preparing the literary landscape for new approaches. The poetry to come. And what, reader, is in store for you? Among the highlights:

Yu Jian's fascination with New York, the twin towers, Ron Padgett, and Ulysses.

Xi Chuan's mix of fairy tale and philosophy and his demand "that turnips, bok choy, and I all be in thought / together..."

Shu Ting's internationalism and political grief.

The grammatically simple, animist, weird jack-in-the-box magic of Gu Cheng's poems.

The clausal layering and multiple voices of Zhou Zan's poems.

Zhai Yongming's tremulous, inward acknowledgment that "Living for the sake of living, I seek my own destruction..."

A glossary list by Huang Fan.

Wang Jiaxin's subtle portrait of the abyss between father and son (so evocative of W.S. Merwin's poem "Yesterday").

Slapdash collisions of cultures and linguistic registers in Hu Xudong's marvelous lyricism.

The poets included in this anthology have worked in factories, in editorial houses, on farms, in universities. Some have lived outside China. Some have committed suicide. Almost all of them steeped themselves in translations of poetry from abroad; some translate or edit or write criticism. Drawing from fresh sources, from a sense of their place in an international community, they are making Chinese poetry new. And, happily for those of us who don't read Chinese, Copper Canyon is making that body of work available to English-language readers.

• • •

A few years ago, I was in Beijing to participate on a panel charged with considering "Where Is Chinese Poetry Going in the Age of Globalization." In a smoke-filled conference room, such an abstract question invites mostly phatic and long-winded, if animated, responses. Yet, better than any argument, this anthology, *Push Open the Window* (along with Zhang Er's *Another Kind of Nation: An Anthology of Contemporary Chinese Poetry* and Arthur Sze's *Chinese Writers on Writing*), begins to provide a capacious and nuanced answer. *Here* is a thrilling slice of Chinese poetry in the Age of Globalization. Open wide.

PUSH OPEN THE WINDOW

相信未来

当蜘蛛网无情地查封了我的炉台
当灰烬的余烟叹息着贫困的悲哀
我依然固执地铺平失望的灰烬
用美丽的雪花写下：相信未来

当我的紫葡萄化为深秋的泪水
当我的鲜花依偎在别人的情怀
我依然固执地用凝露的枯藤
在凄凉的大地上写下：相信未来

我要用手指那涌向天边的排浪
我要用手掌那托起太阳的大海
摇曳着曙光那枝温暖漂亮的笔杆
用孩子的笔体写下：相信未来

我之所以坚定地相信未来
是我相信未来人们的眼睛

Shi Zhi

Shi Zhi, whose real name is Guo Lusheng, was born in 1948 in Shandong and was catapulted to fame when his poems were memorized by the "rusticated youth" during the first years of the Cultural Revolution. His poetry became a major influence on the central members of the so-called Misty School and was prominently featured in the first issue of the journal *Today*. In the late 1980s, Shi Zhi began a thirty-year battle with mental illness that resulted in long stretches (a decade in one case) in several Beijing mental institutions. Married in 2002, Shi Zhi returned to society and has enjoyed a resurgent popularity with older and younger Chinese readers alike.

Translated by Jonathan Stalling

BELIEVE IN THE FUTURE

As spiderwebs mercilessly seal off my stovetop
As smoldering cinders sigh over the sorrows of poverty
I still stubbornly spread out the hopeless cinders
And write with fine flakes of snow: believe in the future

As my purple grapes dissolve into late autumn tears
As my flower leans upon another's breast
I still stubbornly reach for a frozen, withered vine
And write upon the desolate ground: believe in the future

With fingers surging like waves beyond the horizon
I want to hold the sun above the ocean in my palms
With dawn's first flickering rays on my warm, fine pen
I write with a child's hand: believe in the future

I firmly believe in the future because
I have faith in the future of humanity's eyes

她有拨开历史风尘的睫毛
她有看透岁月篇章的瞳孔

不管人们对于我们腐烂的皮肉
那些迷途的惆怅、失败的苦痛
是寄予感动的热泪、深切的同情
还是给以轻蔑的微笑、辛辣的嘲讽

我坚信人们对于我们的脊骨
那无数次的探索、迷途、失败和成功
一定会给予热情、客观、公正的评定
是的，我焦急地等待着他们的评定

朋友，坚定地相信未来吧
相信不屈不挠的努力
相信战胜死亡的年轻
相信未来，热爱生命

1968，北京

这是四点零八分的北京

这是四点零八分的北京，
一片手的海洋翻动；
这是四点零八分的北京，
一声尖厉的汽笛长鸣。

北京车站高大的建筑，
突然一阵剧烈地抖动。
我吃惊地望着窗外，
不知发生了什么事情。

我的心骤然一阵疼痛，一定是
妈妈缀扣子的针线穿透了心胸。

Her eyelashes will push aside the harrowing history
And her pupils will pierce the chapters of time

Regardless of how others will treat our rotting flesh
The grief of losing one's way and the pain of failure
With their moving tears and deep sympathy
Or their contemptuous sneers and caustic scorn

I firmly believe in the backbone of our humanity
The numerous searches, lost ways, successes and failures
Will give us warm, objective, and fair judgment
Yes, I anxiously await their pronouncement

Friend, please firmly believe in the future
Believe in the never-ending struggle
Believe in death-conquering youth
Believe in the future, and love life

1968, Beijing

THIS IS BEIJING AT 4:08

This is Beijing at 4:08
An ocean of waving hands
This is Beijing at 4:08
A shrill train whistle trailing off

Beijing Station's majestic edifice
Convulses without warning
Shaken, I look out the window
Not knowing what's going on

My heart shudders in pain, clearly it is
My mother's needlework running me through

这时，我的心变成了一只风筝，
风筝的线绳就在妈妈手中。

线绳绷得太紧了，就要扯断了，
我不得不把头探出车厢的窗棂。
直到这时，直到这个时候，
我才明白发生了什么事情。

——阵阵告别的声浪，
　　就要卷走车站；
　　北京在我的脚下，
　　已经缓缓地移动。

我再次向北京挥动手臂，
想一把抓住她的衣领，
然后对她大声地叫喊：
永远记着我，妈妈啊北京！

终于抓住了什么东西，
管他是谁的手，不能松，
因为这是我的北京，
这是我的最后的北京。

1968，12，20

At this time my heart transforms into a kite
A kite tethered to her hands

So tight, it may snap
I must stick my head out the train window
Up till now, till this very moment
I understand what has happened

    A fit of parting yells
    Is about to sweep away the train station
    Beijing underfoot
    Slowly begins to move away

Once more I wave to Beijing
And want to grab at her collar
And shout to her
Never forget me
    Mother Beijing!

I've grasped something at last
Who cares whose hand it is—I can't let go!
For this is my Beijing
This is my last Beijing

                        20 December 1968

天空

1

太阳升起来
天空血淋淋的
犹如一块盾牌

2

日子像囚徒一样被放逐
没有人来问我
没有人宽恕我

3

我始终暴露着
只是把耻辱
用唾沫盖住

Mang Ke

Mang Ke, whose real name is Jiang Shiwei, was born in 1950. He began writing poetry in the 1970s and, together with the poet Bei Dao, later launched the literary magazine *Today*. He has published six collections of poetry, one novel, and a volume of essays. His works have been translated into several languages. He lives in Beijing.

Translated by Yibing Huang
and Jonathan Stalling

SKY

1
The sun rises
The sky is blood-soaked
Like a shield

2
Days are banished like prisoners
No one comes to ask me
No one forgives me

3
I am always exposed
With only spit
To cover the shame

4

天空，天空
把你的疾病
从共和国的土地上扫除干净

5

可是，希望变成泪水
掉在地上
我们怎么能够确保明天的人们不悲伤

6

我遥望着天空
我属于天空
天空呵
你提醒着
那向我走来的世界

7

为什么我在你面前走过
总会感到羞怯
好像我老了
我拄着棍子
过去的青春终于落在手中
我拄着棍子
天空
你要把我赶到哪里去
我为了你才这样力尽精疲

4

Sky, sky
Sweep your diseases
Completely off the soil of the Republic

5

Yet, hope turns to tears
Falls to the ground
How can we make sure tomorrow's people won't feel sorrow

6

I look out into the sky
I belong to the sky
O sky
You remind me of
The world walking toward me

7

Why am I always shy
When I pass in front of you
As if I were old
I lean on a cane
Departed youth finally falls into my hand
I lean on a cane
Sky
Where are you driving me
I have exhausted myself only for you

8

谁不想把生活编织成花篮
可是，美好被打扫得干干净净
我们这么年轻
你能否愉悦着我们的眼睛

9

带着你的温暖
带着你的爱
再用你的绿舟
将我远载

10

希望
请你不要去得太远
你在我身边
就足以把我欺骗

11

太阳升起来
天空——这血淋淋的盾牌

1973

阳光中的向日葵

你看到了吗
你看到阳光中的那棵向日葵了吗
你看它，它没有低下头
而是把头转向身后
它把头转了过去

8

Who doesn't want to weave life into a flower basket
Yet, beauty has been swept completely away
We are so young
Can you enchant our eyes

9

Bring your warmth
Bring your love
And use your green boat
To carry me far away

10

Hope
Please don't go too far
Staying by my side
Is enough to keep me deceived

11

The sun rises
The sky—a blood-soaked shield

1973

SUNFLOWER IN THE SUN

Do you see
Do you see that sunflower in the sun
You see, it doesn't bow its head
But turns its head back
It turns its head

就好像是为了一口咬断
那套在它脖子上的
那牵在太阳手中的绳索

你看到它了吗
你看到那棵昂着头
怒视着太阳的向日葵了吗
它的头几乎已把太阳遮住
它的头即使是在没有太阳的时候
也依然在闪耀着光芒

你看到那棵向日葵了吗
你应该走近它
你走近它便会发现
它脚下的那片泥土
每抓起一把
都一定会攥出血来

1983

死后也还会衰老

地里已长出死者的白发
这使我相信：人死后也还会衰老

人死后也还会有恶梦扑在身上
也还会惊醒，睁眼看到

又一个白天从蛋壳里出世
并且很快便开始忙于在地上啄食

也还会听见自己的脚步
听出自己的双腿在欢笑在忧愁

As if to bite through
The rope around its neck
Held by the sun's hands

Do you see it
Do you see that sunflower, raising its head
Glaring at the sun
Its head almost eclipses the sun
Yet even when there is no sun
Its head still glows

Do you see that sunflower
You should get closer to it
Get close and you'll find
The soil beneath its feet
Each handful of soil
Will ooze blood

1983

ONE WILL STILL GROW OLD
EVEN AFTER DEATH

The white hair of the dead grows out of the ground
Which leads me to believe: one will still grow old even after death

One will still be pounced on by nightmares even after death
Will still snap awake, opening eyes only to see

Another day hatches from its shell
And immediately begins busily pecking the ground

Will still hear one's own footsteps
Hear one's own legs laughing and brooding

也还会回忆，尽管头脑里空洞洞的
尽管那些心里的人们已经腐烂

也还会歌颂他们，歌颂爱人
用双手稳稳地接住她的脸

然后又把她小心地放进草丛
看着她笨拙地拖出自己性感的躯体

也还会等待，等待阳光
最后像块破草席一样被风卷走

等待日落，它就如同害怕一只猛兽
会撕碎它的肉似的躲开你

而夜晚，它却温顺地让你拉进怀里
任随你玩弄，发泄，一声不吭

也还会由于劳累就地躺下，闭目
听着天上群兽在争斗时发出的吼叫

也还会担忧，或许一夜之间
天空的血将全部流到地上

也还会站起来，哀悼一副死去的面孔
可她的眼睛还在注视着你

也还会希望，愿自己永远地活着
愿自己别是一只被他人猎取的动物

被放进火里烤着，被吞食
也还会痛苦，也还会不堪忍受啊

地里已经长出死者的白发
这使我相信：人死后也还会衰老

1985

Will still recall, even if the head is empty
Even if loved ones have already decomposed

Will still sing about them, sing of one's lover
Hold her face steadily in both hands

And carefully place her in the grass
Watching her awkwardly drag out her sexy body

Will still wait, wait for sunlight
To be blown away in the end like a frayed straw mat

Wait for sunset, it will hide from you as if fearing a beast
That would tear its flesh asunder

But night, it will meekly let you pull it into your arms
Let you fondle it, ravage it, and not make a sound

Will still lie down exhausted, eyes closed
Listening to the howls of beasts fighting in the sky

Will still worry, perhaps overnight
The blood of the sky will be entirely dumped on the ground

Will still stand up, mourning a dead face
Yet her eyes are still staring at you

Will still hope, wishing oneself to live forever
Wishing oneself not to be an animal hunted by others

Roasted in fire, devoured
Will still feel pain, will still be unable to bear it

The white hair of the dead grows out of the ground
Which leads me to believe: one will still grow old even after death

1985

天职

某一天我起了个绝早
沿海边跑得又轻松又柔韧
我想要消减我的中年
有如消减军事开支
全凭心血来潮 且
不能持之以恒

污秽的沙滩令我联想
非洲水源枯竭
河马坐毙于泥潭
逃难的塞族妇女与儿童
伊拉克饿着肚子
印度焚烧新娘
东北干旱 云南地震
唉 我居住的城市
低温阴雨已有许多天

垃圾车辚辚从身后驶过
不知开往何处

Shu Ting

Shu Ting was born in 1952 and currently resides on Gulang Island, Xiamen City, in Fujian Province. She has been writing poetry since 1969 and was one of the most important members of the Menglong (Misty) Poets, a group that was extremely influential in the 1980s. Since 1998 her most important works have been prose pieces and essays. Her poetry and prose have garnered numerous awards and have been translated into more than a dozen languages.

Translated by Joseph R. Allen
(with Ji Hao)

HIGHER DUTY

Very early one morning I got up
To go jogging along the shore, relaxed and agile
Hoping to reduce my middle age
Like cutting military expenditures
All up to pure whim and with
No real follow-through

The filthy beach reminded me
Of water-depleted Africa
With hippos stuck in mud waiting to die
Of Serbian women and children fleeing disaster
Empty stomachs in Iraq
And burning brides in India
Of the drought in Manchuria... the earthquake in Yunnan
But here in the city where I live
Days of clouds, rain, and sinking temperatures

A garbage truck rattles on by
Off to who knows where

埋在深坑？
运往公海？
最好将辐射物资
装填成飞船射向宇宙
呀呀　就怕日后我的孙子们
不识牛郎织女星
唯见满天旋转垃圾桶

顺路去黄家渡市场
买两斤鸡蛋半个西瓜
恨那菜贩子不肯杀价
趁其不备抓了几根葱
某一天我自觉
履行联合国秘书长的职责
为世界和平操心个不停

也没忘了
给儿子做碗葱花鸡蛋汤

1996，3，21

享受宁静

不能唤回鸽子们我任由鸽巢空虚
天刚向晚　别人的翅膀
焦急着到处留下擦痕
我享受宁静并且震惊于
斜阳撤出叶丛像胶布撕离伤口
树们疼痛的表情　以及
一只在窗玻璃前百折不挠的苍蝇

夏天在五月总是调不准弦
忽而灿烂明亮忽而忧郁低沉

To dump its load in some ditch
Or send it out into the open sea?
Perhaps radioactive waste should be rocketed
Out into the cosmos
But, no, then my grandsons
Could not make out the stars Herdboy and Weaving Maid
From all the orbiting trash bins

On my way home, I stop by the market at Huangjia Ferry
To buy a dozen eggs and half a watermelon
Miffed that the greengrocer will not cut me a deal
I pocket some green onions when he is not looking
I might someday be carrying out my duties
As Secretary-General of the United Nations
Devoting myself completely to world peace

Even so, I did not forget
To make egg-drop soup with green onions for my son

21 March 1996

A PEACEFUL MOMENT

Unable to call the pigeons back in, I let their roosts lie empty
As day shades into night   the wings of others
Leave frantic scratch marks everywhere
Enjoying this peaceful moment, I am shocked
To see the evening light pulling out of the leaves like a bandage ripped
        off a wound
The hurt expression of the trees   and
The fly that keeps throwing itself against the windowpane

The month of May can't keep summer in tune
Once glorious and bright, then suddenly dark and depressing

来回即兴八度跳跃
柏林的身子半边太烫半边太凉
很多人花粉过敏
我仔细把椅子调个方向，当
一只狗在我的影子里抬起后腿

一不留神就纵容语言
熙熙攘攘沸出去蜇人
宁静这张薄纸终于包不住火
属于我的日照越来越短
谁能平衡一棵树
在神话里的兴旺与没落
现在是我隔着玻璃
一再俯冲而碰得头破血流

1996，6

Octaves leaping frantically back and forth
Half the body of Berlin is too hot, half too cool
And many suffer from allergies
I carefully adjust the direction of the chair   as
A dog lifts its hind leg in my shadow

My wandering mind gives words free rein
Gushing forth in a stream to sting people
The tissue of this peaceful moment cannot in the end enfold the flames
This sunlight of mine grows shorter and shorter
Who can balance a tree
Within the rise and fall of myths
Now I am the one on the other side of the window
Again and again, crashing my head into the glass, bruised and bleeding

June 1996

一枚穿过天空的钉子

一直为帽子所遮蔽　直到有一天
帽子腐烂　落下　它才从墙壁上突出
那个多年之前　把它敲进墙壁的动作
似乎刚刚停止　微小而静止的金属
露在墙壁上的秃顶正穿过阳光
进入它从未具备的锋利
在那里　它不只穿过阳光
也穿过房间和它的天空
它从实在的　深的一面
用秃顶　向空的　浅的一面　刺进
这种进入和天空多么吻合
和简单的心多么吻合
一枚穿过天空的钉子
像一位刚刚登基的君王
锋利　辽阔　光芒四射

1996

Yu Jian

Yu Jian, born in 1954, left school at the age of twelve, when the Cultural Revolution began. He worked for ten years as a laborer and entered college in 1980, graduating with a degree in Chinese literature in 1984. He has published prolifically, with much of his work reprinted in a five-volume collection of poems, essays, criticism, and photography from the years 1975 through 2000.

Translated by Cindy M. Carter

THE NAIL THAT PIERCED THE SKY

hidden from view by a hat   until one day
the hat rotted   and fell   the nail sticks out at last
as if the movement that drove it into the wall   all those years ago
has just now ceased   a tiny, static, bald metallic
head juts from the wall, piercing sunlight
with a sharpness   it never knew it possessed
in that place   it passes not only into the light
but into the room, into its own bit of sky
rooted in the deep end   of reality
it cranes its neck   toward the shallow end   of emptiness
    and stabs through
such penetration is a perfect fit with sky
a perfect merging of a simple heart
the nail that pierced the sky
is like a monarch who has just ascended the throne
keen   expansive   radiant in all directions

1996

登纽约帝国大厦

一个被忘掉的日期
排着队
警察盯着　担心你把泥巴带上来
仪器检查完毕　帝国就安全了
电梯满载　升向８６层
圣人登泰山而小鲁
群众去巴黎　要爬埃菲尔铁塔
在纽约　每个裁缝都登过帝国大厦
门票是１２美圆
被一条直线抛了上去
几分钟　未来到了
一个平台将大家截住
全世界有多少人憧憬着这儿
赞美之声　来自高山　平原
来自河流　沼泽地　来自德国的咸肉
北京烤鸭　巴尔干奶酪
红脖子的南美鹦鹉　非洲之鼓
美女们　你们的一生就此可以开始
有一位鞋帮绽线的先生忽然
在出口停下捂住胃部　按实了
深藏在怀中的绿卡
哦　谢天谢地
他的口音有点像尤利西斯
帝国之巅是一个水泥秃顶
所有高速路的终端　几根毛
分别是纪念品商店　卫生间和旗帜
在铁栏杆的保护下
面对秋天的云
如此巨大的脸
经不住一阵风
纽约露出来
工业的野兽
反自然地生长着

EMPIRE STATE

queuing up
on a forgotten date
policemen stare   worried you'll track mud inside
once you've passed the metal detectors   the empire is secure
an elevator, crowded to capacity   rises 86 floors
from this height, the empire seems small
when the masses visit Paris   they climb the Eiffel Tower
in New York   every lowly tailor has been up the Empire State
for $12 admission
you are catapulted skyward
intercepted at the observation deck
in minutes   the future has arrived
how many people in the world have longed for this?
its praises   ring from mountains   plains
waterways   marshlands   from German sausage links
Peking ducks   rounds of Balkan cheese
red-breasted Amazonian parrots   African drums
beauties of the world   *now is where your lives begin*
a gent in tattered, split-seamed shoes stops
at the exit, clutches his gut   a spot-check
on a tucked-away green card
oh thank heavens, it's safe   he sighs
in accents not unlike Ulysses's
the empire's peak is bald concrete
the terminus of all expressways   a few stray hairs
space differentiated into souvenir shops   restrooms and flags
from behind protective guardrails
we gaze at the autumn clouds
their mammoth visage
cannot withstand the wind
and New York City is revealed:
beast of industry
unnatural growth

无数的物积累到这儿
已经空无一物
大地上没有可以比拟它的事物
墓碑林立……这个比方是最接近的
腐烂就是诞生 但这是谁的墓
四个季节过去了 没有长出一根草
先天的抑郁症
啊 可怕的美已经造出来了
隐喻无能为力 无法借鉴历史
也许可以像一辆工程车的方向盘那样
描述它 用几何学 用材料手册
用工具论 用侦探手段 用抛光法
用红绿灯和……一场同性相恋的车祸
纽约 你属于我不知道的知识
哦 纽约 男性之城
欺天的积木 一万座玻璃阳具
刺着 高耸着 炫耀着
抽象的物理学之光
星星变黑 月亮褪色 太阳落幕
时光是一块谄媚的抹布
一切都朝着更高 更年轻
更辉煌 更灿烂 更硬
永恒的眼前一亮
犹如股票市场的指数柱
日夜攀升 更高才是它的根
天空亘古未有地恐惧
这乌龟可不会更高了
取代它的已经君临
飞机像中风的鸟 双翼麻木
从A座飞向B座 最后一点知觉
保证它不会虚拟自己最危险的一面
朝着痴呆的金融之王撞上去
摩天大楼的缝隙里爬着小汽车
这些铁蚂蚁是下面 唯一
在动 令人联想到生命的东西

accretion of innumerable things
all long since empty
nothing on earth compares to it
a forest of tombstones... is the analogy that comes closest
yes, decay is rebirth   but whose tombs are these?
seasons pass   without a single blade of grass
congenital depression
oh what fearsome beauty has been wrought here!
before it, metaphor is powerless   history holds no lessons
maybe think of it as a great construction machine
describe it   with geometry   manuals, reams of data
instrumentalism   applied investigative techniques   methods
        of buff and grind
traffic lights, and... a same-sex car crash
New York   you are my terra incognita
a masculine metropolis
building blocks invading sky   10,000 glass phalluses
pricking   towering   flaunting
the light of an abstract physics
stars go black   moonlight fades   sunshine's curtain falls
burnished by time, that sycophantic rag
everything is trending higher   taller   younger
more splendid   more brilliant   harder
gleaming in perpetuity
like the stock market index
climbing higher day by day   taking "higher" as its baseline
never has the sky known such fear
this tortoise can go no higher
its successor has already taken the throne
an airplane, like a bird   stroking midflight
both wings fixed and paralytic
flies from Tower One to Tower Two   its last conscious moment
proves it incapable of envisioning imminent danger
as it collides with the doddering King of Finance
cars crawling between crevices of skyscrapers
those tiny ants below   are the only things

它们还不够牢固　太矮　流于琐碎
尽管屹立于历史之外　古代的风
经过时　这个立体帝国也还是要
短暂地晕眩　风吹得倒的只有
头发　三个写诗的小人物
还没有垮掉　在巨颅上探头探脑
福州吕德安　纽约帕特　昆明于坚
一游到此　不指点江山
不崇拜物　但要激扬文字
大地太遥远了　看起来就像
天堂　帕特为我们指他的家
他住在一粒尘埃里
永远长不大的格林威治
疮疤　小酒馆　烟嘴
不设防的裙子　有绰号的橡树
金斯堡的沾水钢笔患着梦游症
天一黑就令警棍发疯
尿骚味的地铁车站总是比过去好闻
吸引着年轻人　忧伤而美丽的大麻交易
危险分子在黑暗中交头接耳就像
革命时代的情人　各种枪暗藏着光芒
电话亭子隔板上的血痕属于六十年代
上演韵事的防火梯永不谢幕　哦
弹吉他的总是泪流满面的叔叔　那个黑人
还在流浪　居然还有美人爱上穷鬼
圣马克教堂一直开着门　那地区
有三千个风华正茂者　称自己为
光荣的诗人　一块牛排躺在
祖母留下的煎锅里　有些经典的糊味
太小　尘埃中的灰
完全隐匿在地面了

still moving   the sole reminders of life
but they're untethered   too short   trapped in their own triviality
though it towers outside of history   ancient winds
passing through   can throw this three-dimensional empire
into a momentary tailspin   the only thing blown over
is hair   the three insignificant figures, poets
have not collapsed   three heads protrude from a giant skull
Lü De'an of Fuzhou   Ron Padgett of New York   Yu Jian of
        Kunming
we came here   not to find fault
or to worship at the altar of things   but to inspire with words
the earth, too far below   from here it looks
like heaven   Padgett points out his home
he inhabits a speck of dust
in a Greenwich Village that never grew up
scars   bars   cigarette holders
skirts that put up no defenses   oaks with nicknames
Ginsberg's somnambulist quill
darkness that sends police batons into a frenzy
urine-soaked subway stations that smell better than before
attracting young people   and the mournful, lovely marijuana trade
dangerous elements whispering in the darkness like
lovers in an age of revolution   the concealed gleam of assorted
        firearms
sixties-era bloodstains on the walls of telephone booths
fire escapes upon which trysts were staged   and no curtain call, alas
the old guitarist still sobs as he strums   the black man
remains homeless   beautiful girls still fall for bums
Saint Mark's Cathedral never closes its doors   the neighborhood
        is home
to 3,000 individuals in the prime of life   all self-proclaimed
great poets   a slab of beefsteak reclines
in grandma's hand-me-down frying pan   the classic smell of
        charred meat
too faint   but ashes among the dust
concealed on the ground

更远处　大海之背光芒幽暗
不知道什么时候转过去了
帝国大厦　上来是一种荣耀
下去就随便了　没有光
免费　也不搜身

2005

more distant still, the ocean   light fades upon its back
when, exactly, did it turn away?
Empire State   ascent confers a certain glory
but descent is a casual affair   it's dark
free of charge   and there's no body search

2005

母亲

无力到达的地方太多了，脚在疼痛，母亲，你没有
教会我在贪婪的朝霞中染上古老的哀愁。我的心只像你

你是我的母亲，我甚至是你的血液在黎明流出的血泊中
使你惊讶地看到你自己，你使我醒来

听到这世界的声音，你让我生下来，你让我与不幸构成
这世界的可怕的双胞胎。多年来，我已记不得今夜的哭声

那使你受孕的光芒，来得多么遥远，多么可疑，站在生与死
之间，你的眼睛拥有黑暗　而进入脚底的阴影何等沉重

Zhai Yongming

Zhai Yongming was born in Chengdu, Sichuan, in 1955. As a teenager during the Cultural Revolution, she spent time in a village. Her earliest poems were published in 1981; her first collection appeared four years later, and many more books have followed. Her style continues to evolve, and she is active in women's poetry and in the arts. She co-owns a bar in Chengdu called White Nights, which has functioned for over a decade as an informal salon for local writers and artists.

Translated by Andrea Lingenfelter

MOTHER

There are too many places I lack the strength to reach, my feet are
     aching. Mother, you didn't
Teach me to bear the taint of ancient grief in the greed of rosy dawns.
     My heart resembles only you

You are my mother, and I your blood in the pool that flowed out at
     daybreak
Startled to see yourself, you awakened me

To hear the sounds of this world, you brought me into this life, paired
     me with misfortune into
Twins the world would fear. It's been years since I could recall the
     sound of that night's weeping

The ray of light that impregnated you, so distant in origin, and so
     suspicious, stood between
Life and Death, and your eyes held the darkness, heavy shadows
     penetrated your feet

在你怀抱之中，我曾露出谜底似的笑容，有谁知道
你让我以童贞方式领悟一切，但我却无动于衷

我把这世界当作处女，难道我对着你发出的
爽朗的笑声没有燃烧起足够的夏季吗？没有？

我被遗弃在世上，只身一人，太阳的光线悲哀地
笼罩着我，当你俯身世界时是否知道你遗落了什么？

岁月把我放在磨子里，让我亲眼看见自己被碾碎
呵，母亲，当我终于变得沉默，你是否为之欣喜

没有人知道我是怎样不着痕迹地爱你，这秘密
来自你的一部分，我的眼睛像两个伤口痛苦地望着你

活着为了活着，我自取灭亡，以对抗亘古已久的爱
一块石头被抛弃，直到像骨髓一样风干，这世界

有了孤儿，使一切祝福暴露无遗，然而谁最清楚
凡在母亲手上站过的人，终会因诞生而死去

1984

Held in your arms, I smiled a smile like the answer to a riddle, and who
    could know that
You would lead me so chastely to a knowledge of everything, while I
    remained unmoved

I saw the world as virgin, and when my laughter at you
Rang out, didn't it set enough summers on fire? Didn't it?

Abandoned to the world, I was on my own, rays of sunlight mournfully
Enveloping me, and when you looked down over the world, didn't you
    realize you'd left something behind?

The years put me through a mill, made me watch with my own eyes as
    I was ground to pieces
Oh Mother, when I finally fell silent, did it please you?

No one knows how hard I tried to love you without leaving a trace,
    this secret
Originates from something in you, my eyes like a pair of open wounds
    that watch you and ache

Living for the sake of living, I seek my own destruction, casting a stone
    to repel
That ancient love, drying like marrow in the wind, this world

Has its orphans, bringing every blessing to light, yet who sees
    most clearly
All who have stood in a mother's hand are sure to die because they
    were born

1984

轻伤的人，重伤的城市

轻伤的人过来了
他们的白色纱布像他们的脸
他们的伤痕比战争缝合得好
轻伤的人过来了
担着心爱的东西
没有断气的部分
脱掉军服　洗净全身
使用支票和信用卡

一个重伤的城市血气翻涌
脉搏和体温在起落
比战争快
比恐惧慢
重伤的城市
扔掉了假腿和绷带
现在它已流出绿色分泌物
它已提供石材的万能之能
一个轻伤的人　仰头
看那些美学上的建筑

六千颗炸弹砸下来
留下一个燃烧的军械所
六千颗弹着点
像六千只重伤之眼
匆忙地映照出
那几千个有夫之妇
有妇之夫　和未婚男女的脸庞
他们的身上全是硫磺，或者沥青
他们的脚下是拆掉的钢架

轻伤的人　从此
拿着一本重伤的地图

LIGHTLY INJURED PEOPLE, GRAVELY WOUNDED CITY

Here they come, the lightly injured
Their gauze as white as their faces
Wounds sewn up more neatly than the war
Here they come, the lightly injured
Carrying their prized possessions
The parts that have not died
They strip off their uniforms   they wash themselves clean
Pay by check and credit card

The gravely wounded city seethes with energy
Its pulse and temperature rising and falling
Faster than war
Slower than fear
Gravely wounded city
Casting off its bandages and artificial legs
It has bled a green secretion
And offered the unyielding power of stone
One of the lightly injured   raises his head to look
At those monuments to aesthetics

Six thousand bombs come pounding down
Leaving an armory in flames
Six thousand bombs are blazing
Like six thousand gravely wounded eyes
In a rush they illuminate the faces of
Thousands of married women
Married men   unmarried men and women
Bodies covered in sulfur   or asphalt
And at their feet, twisted metal frames

The lightly injured   now set out
Heavily wounded maps in hand

他们分头去寻找那些
新的器皿大楼
薄形，轻形和尖形
这个城市的脑袋
如今尖锐锋利地伸出去
既容易被砍掉
也吓退了好些伤口

2000，柏林

They split up to search
For the new vessels of tall buildings
Forms thin and light and pointed
The brain of this city
Now extends its spikes
Though easy to hack off
They've scared away my cuts

2000, Berlin

月光白得很

月亮在深夜照出了一切的骨头。

我呼进了它青白的气息。
人间的琐碎皮毛
变成下坠的萤火虫。
城市这具死去了的骨架。

没有哪个生命
配得上这样纯的夜色。
微微打开窗帘
天地正在眼前交接白银
月光使我忘记我是一个人。

生命的最后一幕
在一片素色里静静地彩排。
月光来到地板上
我的两只脚已经预先白了。

Wang Xiaoni

Wang Xiaoni, born in 1955, lives between Shenzhen, Guangdong Province, and Hainan Island. She has published twenty-one volumes of poetry, essays, and fiction over the last two decades. She is a professor in the College of the Humanities and Communications at Hainan University.

Translated by Tze-lan D. Sang

MOONLIGHT, A BRILLIANT WHITE

The shining moon reveals all the bones in the dark of night.

I breathe in its pallid breath.
The frivolities of the mundane world
Turn into falling fireflies.
The city, a lifeless skeleton.

Not a single life
Deserves such pure nocturnal beauty.
I part the drapes slightly
To see heaven and earth communing with white silver,
Forgetful that I am a human being.

The last scene of my life
Rehearses itself in silence, in the total whiteness.
The moonlight reaches the floor.
My feet have already turned pale.

一块布的背叛

我没有想到
把玻璃擦净以后
全世界立刻渗透进来。
最后的遮挡跟着水走了
连树叶也为今后的窥视
纹浓了眉线。

我完全没有想到
只是两个小时和一块布
劳动，忽然也能犯下大错。

什么东西都精通背叛。
这最古老的手艺
轻易地通过了一块柔软的脏布。
现在我被困在它的暴露之中。

别人最大的自由
是看的自由
在这个复杂又明媚的春天
立体主义者走下画布。
每一个人都获得了剖开障碍的神力
我的日子正被一层层看穿。

躲在家的最深处
却袒露在四壁以外的人
我只是裸露无遗的物体。
一张横竖交错的桃木椅子
我藏在木条之内
心思走动。
世上应该突然大降尘土
我宁愿退回到
那桃木的种子之核。

只有人才要隐秘
除了人现在我什么都想冒充。

BETRAYED BY A PIECE OF CLOTH

It did not occur to me
The world would immediately seep in
After the glass was wiped clean.
My last shield was washed away with the water.
Even tree leaves have darkened their eyebrows
To better peep in from now on.

It didn't occur to me at all
That for a mere two hours with a piece of cloth
Physical labor could abruptly lead to such a huge mistake.

Everything is an expert in the art of betrayal.
This most ancient craft
Had no difficulty passing through a soft dirty cloth.
I'm now trapped in its exposure.

Others' greatest freedom
Is the freedom to look.
In this complicated and gorgeous springtime
The cubists are walking off their canvases.
Everyone is gaining the magical power to cut through obstructions
My days are being seen through, layer by layer.

Hiding in the deepest corner of the house
Yet exposed beyond the walls
I'm but a naked object not a person.
A chair of horizontal and vertical lines made of peach wood
I hide in the wood slats
My mind wandering.
A gigantic sandstorm should swiftly descend to earth.
I'd rather return
To the kernel of the peach's seed.

Only humans need privacy.
Right now I want to pretend to be anything but human.

登首象山诗札之二

一日一变。今日之山已非十天前；
菊花已半枯，草之绿色已变成紫色。
在上山途中碰上摘柿子的农民，
解决了心里疑问；葡萄般晶莹的果子，
不过是另一种柿子——登山也是学习。
尤其是站在峰顶，再一次远眺，
看见雾霭笼罩的机场乌龟壳一样的屋顶，
心中更加明确什么是人；无论怎样的大欲望，
也大不过大地。所以，应该让内心像天空一样，
最好只呈现一片空洞的蓝色；
然后，感觉进入比空洞更绝对的虚无
——只有虚无是永恒的。就像看不见的风，
让每一棵树、每一株草、每一朵花发出声音，
成为充满奥秘的音乐。听，成为向没有致敬；
——致敬岩石；构成陡峭山势的岩石，
没有生命却拥有不朽；没有变化，
却成为变化的见证——相比我们总是
期待文字成为见证。但是，又能见证什么？

Sun Wenbo

Sun Wenbo was born in 1956 in Chengdu, Sichuan. He began writing poetry in 1985 and has since published half a dozen collections.

Translated by Christopher Lupke

ON CLIMBING SHOUXIANG MOUNTAIN NUMBER 2

A change a day. Today's mountain is no longer the one of ten days ago;
The chrysanthemum flowers are half withered,
The green of the grass has changed to purple.
Climbing the mountain, we met some farmers picking persimmons,
Relieving any doubts in the mind, the fruit glistening like grapes,
They're just a different kind of persimmon—climbing the mountain is
        also a learning experience.
Especially when one stands on the peak, with another chance to gaze
        far in the distance,
Watching the mist-enshrouded airport with its rooftops like tortoise
        shells,
It's much clearer what a person is; no matter how big one's desire
        might be,
It can't be bigger than the vast land. So one should make one's mind
        like the sky,
The best thing would be for it to become a hollow blue;
Then feelings enter an emptiness more absolute than the hollowness
—Only emptiness is eternal. Like the invisible wind,
Making every tree, each blade of grass, and every flower emit sound,
Creating a mystical music. Listening becomes a homage to the nothing
—A homage to the crag; forming a sheer, mountainous cliff,
It has no life but possesses immortality; it will not change,
But is a witness to change—compared to us who must always
Look to language to be our witness. But what can we witness?

当我写橡子壳、绒球草；当我写下山的
途中，碰上开着宝马来登山的一家人。

登首象山诗札之三（为柳宗宣、阿西来访而作）

登山，不是为了看风景，也不是
为了锻炼身体。登山，是寻找一首诗。
它可能是残存的积雪，干枯的落叶，
和叫不上名字的各种灌木，还有突然飞起的
全身褐色的野鸡。但它们都比不上山顶的风；
它飞镖一样刮过耳边，就像在给与你
诗的节奏：必须强烈，必须刺激人的耳膜
——不要说，还真是有用，一下子你就找到了
应该怎样遣词造句，应该让什么物象入诗
——孤独、沉默，面对苍凉；或者：转换、偏离，
人也是树。你让这些构成一个整体。让它们要么
表示内心的图像，要么传达世界的声音。
而我由此看到，任何时候，都必须扼制轻慢之心，
对每一种事物有敬畏的态度——是的！
怎么能不这样呢？就像这山上的每一块岩石，
每一棵树，甚至看林人居住的六角形小楼，
它们的存在就是大地的见证——见证我们向远方
眺望——氤氲的雾气笼罩下，所有的建筑
都像漂浮物，犹如在未知中远航，却又不知
会驶向何处——我和你当然也是……这样。

When I write of an acorn, of the meadow grass, when I write of
    descending
A mountain, running into a family driving their BMW as they make
    the climb.

ON CLIMBING SHOUXIANG MOUNTAIN NUMBER 3 (AFTER A VISIT FROM LIU ZONGXUAN AND AH XI)

Climbing a mountain is not done to view the scenery, and it's not done
For exercise. Climbing a mountain is done to find a poem.
It might be in the remnants of a snow pile, some dried-out, fallen leaves,
Or some shrubs nobody knows the name of, or it could be in a
    pheasant, brown all over,
That suddenly gives flight. But none of these can match the wind on
    the mountaintop.
Slicing by one's ear like a dart, as if providing the rhythm
For your poem: it must be intense, it must stimulate a person's eardrum.
Needless to say, it's also really useful, in a flash you figure out how
    you should
Word it and put together the lines, what images you should include in it:
Loneliness, silence, facing desolation; or: change, divergence,
People are trees, too. You make this into a whole. You either make
    them depict
An image of your interior world or you convey the sounds of the world.
And thus I realize, no matter when, I must still the arrogant heart,
I must maintain a reverent attitude toward all things—yes!
How could I be otherwise? Just like every crag on this mountain,
Like every tree, even like the hexagonal cottages of the foresters
Whose existence is a witness to the land—witnessing us
Gaze into the distance—enshrouded in the mistiness of fog, all the
    buildings
Like flotsam, as if on a long voyage to an unknown location, and not
    knowing
Where they are sailing to—like you, I of course am, too... just like this.

生日

因为生日
我得到了一个彩色钱夹
我没有钱
也不喜欢那些乏味的分币

我跑到那个古怪的大土堆后
去看那些爱美的小花
我说：我有一个仓库了
可以用来贮存花籽

Gu Cheng

Gu Cheng loved life even as a child. Enthralled by beauty, he was sensitive to the tiniest and grandest of natural and humanistic landscapes. A passionate devotee of poetry, painting, and music, he was relatively slow in reacting to norms and procedural issues. He began writing poetry consciously though aimlessly in his early teens, his output peaking in the countryside during the Cultural Revolution; he became a well-known poet in 1979. In May 1987, he left China for Germany. From January 1988 to June 1990 he taught at the University of Auckland in New Zealand, during which time he moved to an island (in July 1988), where he practiced a lifestyle of self-reliance. In March 1992 he went to work in Germany. Currently there are over two thousand poems available in complete form, essays totaling two to three million characters, and several hundred paintings.*

Translated by Richard King

BIRTHDAY

For my birthday
I received a colorful change-purse
I have no money
And no fondness for drab coins

I ran behind the strange hillock
To look at flowers that love beauty
I said: now I have a storehouse
I can use to collect seeds from these flowers

---

* Translation co-editors' note: We would like to acknowledge the family of Gu Cheng (1956–1993) for providing this biographical note.

钱夹里真的装满了花籽
有的黑亮黑亮
像奇怪的小眼睛
我又说：别怕
我要带你们到春天的家里去
在那儿，你们会得到
绿色的短上衣
和彩色花边的布帽子

我有一个小钱夹了
我不要钱
不要那些不会发芽的分币
我只要装满小小的花籽
我要知道她们的生日

1981，12

有天

总有那么一天
阳光都变成叶子
我的路成为宫殿
每块石头都可以住一住
那里的花纹
　　最大的画家都惊叹

总有那么一天
叶子都变成阳光
我的木台升到天上
每个小钉都会讲故事
那里的新奇
　　最小的孩子都入迷

1991，7

The purse is truly packed full of seeds
Some glistening black
Like odd little eyes
Then I said: have no fear
I will take you to the house of springtime
There you will receive
Pea green jackets
And cotton hats with colored brims

I have a little change-purse
I want no money
No drab coins that will not sprout
I want only to pack it with tiny seeds
And know *their* birthdays

December 1981

ONE DAY

There will come a day
When rays of sunlight turn into leaves
My road becomes a palace
Where every pebble can be lived in
Whose patterned stones
    Would make the greatest artists marvel

There will come a day
When the leaves turn into sunlight
My terrace ascends to heaven
Where every nail tells a story
Whose magical novelty
    Would amaze the smallest children

July 1991

要用光芒抚摸

这个岛真好
一树一树花
留下果子

我吃果子
只是为了跟花
有点联系

光没有罪恶
要用光芒抚摸

你把我没入水中
吐出空气
吐出人和树
你让我站到最深的地方
站在柔软凄凉的光上

我知道我的道路
是最美的

1992，1

LET RAYS OF LIGHT CARESS ME

This island is lovely
Every tree a tree in blossom
Hung with fruit

I eat the fruit
Just so I can
Have some affinity with the blossoms

Light has no guilt
Let rays of light caress me

You immerse me in water
Spit out air
Spit out people and trees
You let me stand at the deepest point
Standing on soft dreary light

I know that my path
Is the most beautiful of all

January 1992

夏天还很远

一日逝去又一日
某种东西暗中接近你
坐一坐，走一走
看树叶落了
看小雨下了
看一个人沿街而过
夏天还很远

真快呀，一出生就消失
所有的善在十月的夜晚进来
太美，全不察觉
巨大的宁静如你干净的布鞋
在床边，往事依稀、温婉
如一只旧盒子
一只褪色的书签
夏天还很远

偶然遇见，可能想不起
外面有一点冷
左手也疲倦
暗地里一直往左边

Bai Hua

Bai Hua, born in 1956 in Chongqing, is a professor of art and communications at the Southwest Jiaotong University. He is an outstanding representative of modern China's Third Generation of poets and has published numerous poems in prestigious anthologies and literary magazines as well as several books.

Translated by John Balcom

SUMMER IS STILL VERY FAR AWAY

One day passes after another
Secretly, something approaches you
Sitting, walking
Watching the leaves drop
Watching the rain fall
Watching as someone walks down the street
Summer is still very far away

It happened so fast, vanishing at birth
All that is good entered on an October night
So beautiful, entirely unnoticed
A great serenity like your clean cloth shoes
The past, vague and gentle, lingers at the bedside
Like an old box
A faded bookmark
Summer is still very far away

Meeting by chance, perhaps you can't recall
It was a little cold outside
Your left hand was tired, too
Secretly you walked all the way to the left

偏僻又深入
那唯一痴痴的挂念
夏天还很远

再不了，动辄发脾气，动辄热爱
拾起从前的坏习惯
灰心年复一年
小竹楼、白衬衫
你是不是正当年？
难得下一次决心
夏天还很远

1984冬

望气的人

望气的人行色匆匆
登高眺远
眼中沉沉的暮霭
长出黄金、几何与宫殿

穷巷西风突变
一个英雄正动身去千里之外
望气的人看到了
他激动的草鞋和布衫

更远的山谷浑然
零落的钟声依稀可闻
两个儿童打扫着亭台
望气的人坐对空寂的傍晚

吉祥之云宽大
一个干枯的导师沉默
独自在吐火、炼丹
望气的人看穿了石头里的图案

Far away, deep in
The sole infatuation of your heart
Summer is still very far away

Never again easy to anger, easy to love
To take up those old bad habits of yours
Losing heart with each passing year
A small bamboo house, a white shirt
Are you in the prime of life?
Seldom can a decision be made
Summer is still very far away

winter 1984

THE SEER

The seer is in a hurry to be off
To ascend and gaze into the beyond
The heavy evening mist in his eyes
Out of which grow gold, geometry, and palaces

In a slum lane the west wind suddenly turns
A hero sets off on a journey beyond a thousand miles
The seer sees
His agitated straw sandals and cotton clothes

Farther beyond is the valley in its wholeness
Sporadically, the tolling of a bell is still faintly heard
Two boys sweep the pavilion
The seer sits facing the desolate evening

Auspicious clouds expand
In silence, a withered old master
Alone amid shooting flames, alchemizing
The seer sees through the pattern in a stone

乡间的日子风调雨顺
菜田一畦，流水一涧
这边青翠未改
望气的人已走上了另一座山巅

1986暮春

Rural days of good weather
Ridged rectangular fields, a stream of running water
It's still jade green on this side
The seer is already at the top of another peak

late spring 1986

我该说些什么呢？

我该说些什么呢，面对这无情的世界，
和雪一样的冷漠。小丑们戴着假面
显得兴高采烈。"生活就是快乐，"他们这样说。
而在我看来不是。我实在没有办法快乐。
森林在消失，河流变得干涸。
岁月带来的不是智慧，而是更多的惶惑。
雪总是在下。像冬日午后的闲谈。
但面对真实我无话可说。

呼兰河传

自从第一次见到那条河，混浊
而发黄，因一部小说而知名，
并不湍急，只是懒散地
打了个转，朝着东北方向
缓缓地流淌，已经四十年过去。
我在它的河边长大，另一个
县城，当时我没有读过那本书，
甚至不知道作者的名字。
但我却听过有关它的传说，

Zhang Shuguang

Zhang Shuguang was born in 1956 in Heilongjiang Province. He began writing poetry in college, adopting a robust, hearty style. He has translated into Chinese Dante's *Divine Comedy* and the poetry of Milosz. He teaches literature at a college in Harbin.

Translated by Haowen Ge

WHAT CAN I SAY?

What can I say, in the face of this heartless world
cold and indifferent as snow? Clowns wear masks
seemingly in high spirits. "Life means happiness," they say,
but that's not how I see it. I can never be happy.
Forests are disappearing, rivers are drying up.
The years bring not wisdom but increasing apprehension.
Snow keeps falling. Like small talk on a winter afternoon.
But in the face of truth, I can say nothing.

TALES OF HULAN RIVER

Since my first sight of the river, turbid
yellow, knowing its name from a novel,
flowing lazily, not rushing along,
turning and moving slowly to the northeast,
forty years gone by.
I grew up on its banks, another
county town, before I'd read the novel,
and not knowing who wrote it.
But I'd heard stories about the river, like,

譬如，某位县长杀了他乡下的
发妻，把尸体抛在了河里。
而一场大水，把她的尸体冲到
娘家的门口，就再也不肯离去。
我没有见过那尸体，却看见
淹死的猪，鸡，连同泡沫
和草末，随着河水流向天边。
离县城八里路。那一年
母亲住进了河边的疗养院，
我和弟弟暑假去那里，我们
偷偷在河里撑船，和大人们一起
去起挂网，捕到的鱼，被放进
屋前的水坑，它们可以活上很久，
或被很快烹饪，端上餐桌。
哦，很久了，那个夏天。但我
仍然记得芦苇间的天空——
飘着白云，是那样的宁静——
和微风带来的河水的腥味。
它静静地流着，人们活在
它的两岸，贫穷，快乐
或忧伤。而它见过了太多的
苦难，或死亡。我的两位同学
——小学和中学的——就淹死在里面。
刘娟，据说他的母亲为他起了
女孩的名字，为的是好养活；
另一个叫陈小峰，高高的个子，
漂亮，在今天会被人们称为帅哥。
他应该四十几岁了，如果还活着，
也许会变得大腹便便，像其他人。
而我还活着，体味着死者们
留下的辛酸。太多的死亡和
太多的承载，我将在这里悼念
我的母亲，舅舅，祖母，外祖母，
以及我的两位叔叔，悼念死去的
时间和记忆，悼念这条终将会变得
枯干的河，但它也许还会流上好多年。

a certain County Chief murdered his first wife,
a country girl, threw her body into the river.
Then came a flood, carried her body to
the gate of her family home, and it never left.
I never saw her body, but I've seen
drowned pigs, chickens, entangled in foam
and sodden weeds, floating off to the horizon.
Two miles from the county town. That year
Mother moved into a riverside sanatorium,
my kid brother and I went there on summer break,
sneaking out in a boat to cast nets with the
grown-ups, to catch fish and put them
in a puddle outside, keeping them alive,
or quickly cooking and putting them on the table.
Oh, such a long time, that summer. But I
still recall the sky poking through reeds—
clouds floating by, so peaceful and quiet—
with the rank smell of river on the breezy air.
Silently it flowed, people living
on both banks, poor, happy
or laden with misery. It has witnessed so much
suffering, so much death. Two of my schoolmates
—primary and secondary—drowned in it.
Liu Juan's mother gave him a
girl's name, to keep him from harm, they say;
then there was Chen Xiaofeng, a tall boy,
good-looking, today they'd call him lady-killer.
He would be in his forties, if he'd lived,
might have a paunch like other men.
I'm still around, living with the sorrow
left behind by the dead. So many deaths,
too many to bear. Here is where I mourn
my mother, her brother, grandmothers—both of them
—two of my father's brothers, mourn the passing
of time and of memory, mourn a river bound to
dry up, but maybe not for many years yet.

它是松花江的一条支流，最终
会汇入黑龙江，辗转流进大海。

诗人和柏拉图

在诗人被逐出理想国之后，他们
开始在尘世间流浪。许多年过去，
他们身上的污垢更重，声音
也变得嘶哑。而柏拉图本人也没有
在那里呆上多久，他被但丁安置到了
林菩狱，地狱中最宁静的一层。
现在他可以专心地谈着他的哲学了。
他不开心的是，他讨厌的那些诗人
也住在这里。他们整天吵吵嚷嚷
一会儿吟诵，一会儿追逐女人。

A tributary of the Sungari River, it merges
with the Heilong River, and empties into the sea.

PLATO AND THE POETS

After the poets were banished from Utopia, they
began to roam the world of men. With the passage of years,
they were weighed down with filth, their voices
turned hoarse. But Plato did not
hang around for long. Dante arranged for him a place
in Limbo, Hell's most peaceful level.
Now free to propagate his philosophy.
What made him unhappy was that poets he disliked
were there with him. They quarreled all day long,
chanting one moment, chasing women the next.

田园诗

如果你在京郊的乡村路上漫游
你会经常遇见羊群
它们在田野中散开，像不化的雪
像膨胀的绽开的花朵
或是缩成一团穿过公路，被吆喝着
滚下尘土飞扬的沟渠

我从来没有注意过它们
直到有一次我开车开到一辆卡车的后面
在一个飘雪的下午
这一次我看清了它们的眼睛
（而它们也在上面看着我）
那样温良，那样安静
像是全然不知它们将被带到什么地方
对于我的到来甚至怀有
几分孩子似的好奇

Wang Jiaxin

Wang Jiaxin was born in Danjiangkou, Hubei, in 1957. He was sent down to a farm during the Cultural Revolution, entering Wuhan University when it was over. From 1985 to 1990 he edited the journal *Shikan*. He lived in England from 1992 to 1994 and is now a professor at People's University. He has published a number of books of poetry and several volumes of poetry criticism. He was co-translator into Chinese of *The Poems of Paul Celan*.

Translated by John Balcom

PASTORAL POEM

If you wander the country roads outside the capital
You'll often see flocks of sheep
Spread out over the fields like patches of lingering snow
Like swollen buds bursting into bloom
Or, loudly herded, pressing together, crossing the highway
Rolling down the ditch where the dust rises

I never really paid attention to them
Until I found myself driving behind a truck
On an afternoon as the snow was falling
I clearly saw their eyes that time
(And they were looking down at me)
So calm and so meek
As if oblivious to where they were being taken
Even treating my appearance there
With a child's curiosity

我放慢了车速
我看着它们
消失在愈来愈大的雪花中

2004，12，北京

和儿子一起喝酒

一个年过五十的人还有什么雄心壮志
他的梦想不过是和久别的
已长大的儿子坐在一起喝上一杯
两只杯子碰在一起
这就是他们拥抱的方式
也是他们和解的方式
然后，什么也不说
当儿子起身去要另一杯
父亲，则呆呆地看着杯沿的泡沫
流下杯底。

2007，10

I slowed my car
I watched them
Vanish amid ever-larger snowflakes

December 2004, Beijing

DRINKING WITH HIS SON

What ambitions does a man past fifty still hold
His dream is but to sit and drink a glass of beer
With his long-estranged grown-up son
They clink their glasses together
This is the way they hug
It is also how they are reconciled
Then they say nothing
As the son gets up for another glass
The father stares blankly as the foam on the rim
Slips to the bottom of his glass

October 2007

答问

给费迎晓

1

所以，小姐，一旦我们问："为什么？"
那延宕着的就变成了质疑。
它就像一柄剑在匣中鸣叫着，虽然
佩剑的人还没诞生。迄今为止
诗歌并未超越那尖锐的声音。

2

我们不过是流星。原初的
沉睡着，有待叩问，但岁月匆匆。
当一行文字迷失于雾中，我们身上的逝者
总会适时回来，愤怒地反驳，
或微笑着为我们指点迷津。

3

写作是一扇门，开向原野，
我们的进出也是太阳每天的升降，
有一种恍惚难以抵达。于是秋天走来，

Song Lin

Song Lin, born in 1959 in Xiamen, Fujian Province, has a degree in Chinese from East China Normal University. In 1991, she emigrated from China to settle in France. She has also resided in Singapore and Argentina, and currently teaches at Shenyang Normal University. She has received the Shanghai Literature Award, the Rotterdam International Poetry Festival Award, and other honors.

THE ANSWER

for Fei Yingxiao

translated by Ronald M. Kimmons

1

And so, Miss, whenever we ask "Why?"
what is being delayed turns into a question.
It is like a sword crying out from a box, even though
the sword bearer is not yet born. As of now,
the song has not drowned out the sharp voice.

2

We are but meteors. The primordial
slumbers, awaiting an inquiring knock, but the seasons hurry on.
When one line of text is lost in the haze, the dead we carry
always return in due time, rebuking us angrily
or pointing out the right path with a smile.

3

Writing is a door open into the wilds,
and our coming and going is the sun's daily rising and setting.
There is a dimness that is hard to reach. Thus the fall comes,

涂抹体内的色彩，使它深化，
然后消隐，像火狐的一瞥。

4

这些是差异：过去意味着反复，
未来难以预测；面对着面的人，
陷入大洋的沉默。而风在躯体的边缘
卷曲。风摇着我们，像摇着帆，
不知不觉中完成了过渡。

5

所以我们必须警惕身分不明的，
长久失踪的东西，隶属于更大的传统，
在更远的地方移动，遮蔽在光线中——
真实，像一只准确无误的杯子，
被突然递到我们面前。

秦始皇陵的勘探

七十万奴隶的劳作算得了什么？
在骊山苍翠的一侧，他们挖，他们挖。
再重的巨石终比不上强秦的课税，
撬不起的是公孙龙子的坚白论。

痴迷的考古学家在烈日下勘探，
且为我们复现出，无论过去、现在、
或将来，各种暴君的癖好：
生前的奢华，死后无限的排场。

it paints the body's inner color, intensifying it,
then it disappears, like the glance of a red fox.

      4

These are the differences: the past implies repetition,
and the future is hard to predict; those who face each other
fall into an ocean of silence. Around the body, the wind
curls. The wind rocks us, as with a sail,
and we cross over without knowing it.

      5

So we must beware the unidentified,
that which is long lost, belonging to a greater tradition,
stirring in more distant places, masked in rays of light—
true, like a perfectly crafted glass
that is suddenly placed before us.

EXPLORING THE TOMB OF
THE FIRST EMPEROR

translated by Charles A. Laughlin

Does the labor of seven hundred thousand slaves matter?
On a verdant slope of Mount Li, they dig. They dig.
No boulder, no matter how great, can outweigh the levies of the Qin;
What cannot be pried loose is Master Gongsun Long's "On Hard
      or White."

Obsessed archaeologists explore under the blazing sun,
And resurrect for us—regardless of past, present,
Or future—the tyrant's every whim:
Opulence in life, and unlimited extravagance after death.

七十万奴隶，七十万堆尘土。
上蔡的李斯还能到东门猎几回兔子呢？
阿房宫固然华美，经不住一把火，
肉体的永存有赖于神赐的丹药。

空旷的帝国需要一些东西来填满，
需要坚贞的女人为远征的夫婿而哭泣，
六国亡魂该听得见长城轰然倾颓吧？
该知道，地狱之塔奇怪的倒椎体。

但这深处的死亡宫殿却是有力的矩形！
在令人窒息且揣摩不透的中心，
我猜测，祖龙仍将端坐在屏风前，
等待大臣徐福从遥远的渤海归来。

而机关密布中的弩矢是否仍能射杀？
躬着身，模拟百川和大海的水银，
柔软且安详地熟睡着，一朝醒来，
会不会吐出千年的蛇信啮咬我们？

隔着木然的兵马俑，在相邻的坑道里，
殉葬的宫女和匠人吸进了最后一口空气。
封墓的瞬间，透过逆光，他几乎已经看见，
一只侧身的燕子逃过了灭顶之灾。

2007，2

Seven hundred thousand slaves, seven hundred thousand piles of earth.
Can Li Si of Shangcai still hunt rabbits at East Gate?
Epang Palace, however splendid, could not withstand the torch;
For eternal life, the flesh must rely on god-given elixir.

Vast empires need to be filled with things,
They need chaste women to weep for their distant, conscripted husbands;
The dead of six states should be able to hear the Great Wall's collapse...
They should know the strange inverted cone, the tower of hell.

But this deep palace of the dead is a powerful rectangle!
In its suffocating, unfathomable center,
I suppose, the ancestor of all emperors sits upright before the folding
        screen,
Awaiting the return of Xu Fu from his long journey beyond the Bohai Sea.

And can the arrows in the densely arrayed crossbows still shoot to kill?
Curling in repose, quicksilver, in the form of rivers and seas,
Softly and serenely dozes; on the morning when it wakes,
Will it spew a millennial snake to bite us?

Separated by impassive terra-cotta armies, in a neighboring pit,
Sacrificed palace ladies and artisans breathed their last.
In the moment the tomb was sealed, he could almost already see, backlit,
A sideways-flying swallow narrowly escape its doom.

February 2007

北站

我感到我是一群人。
在老北站的天桥上，我身体里
有人开始争吵和议论，七嘴八舌。
我抽着烟，打量着火车站的废墟，
我想叫喊，嗓子里火辣辣的。

我感到我是一群人。
走在废弃的铁道上，踢着铁轨的卷锈，
哦，身体里拥挤不堪，好像有人上车，
有人下车。一辆火车迎面开来，
另一辆从我的身体里呼啸而出。

我感到我是一群人。
我走进一个空旷的房间，翻过一排栏杆，
在昔日的检票口，突然，我的身体里
空荡荡的。哦，这个候车厅里没有旅客，
站着和坐着的都是模糊的影子。

我感到我是一群人。
在附近的弄堂里，在烟摊上，在公用电话旁，

Xiao Kaiyu

Xiao Kaiyu was born in the Heping Commune in Zhongjiang County, Sichuan, in 1960. In 1979, upon graduation from the Mianyang Medical School in Sichuan, he practiced medicine in his hometown. He has lived and worked in Chengdu, Shanghai, and Berlin, and is currently a professor in the Chinese department at Henan University. He began writing poetry in 1986 and has published several collections.

Translated by Christopher Lupke

NORTH STATION

I felt I was a multitude.
On the skywalk at Shanghai's Old North Station, in my body
People began disputing and deliberating, all clamoring at once.
While smoking, I sized up the train station in ruins,
I felt like screaming, but my throat was scorched.

I felt I was a multitude.
Walking among the abandoned rail lines, kicking the tracks warped
    with rust,
Ah, my body felt jammed, as if people were boarding,
And disembarking. A train was racing toward me,
Another one came howling out of my body.

I felt I was a multitude.
I entered a cavernous room, jumped the railing,
At the ticket window from days past, my body suddenly
Felt vacant. Ah, the station terminal was devoid of travelers,
All that were standing and sitting were murky shadows.

I felt I was a multitude.
In a nearby alleyway, by the cigarette stand, next to the pay phone

他们像汗珠一样出来。他们蹲着，跳着，
堵在我的前面。他们戴着手表，穿着花格衬衣，
提着沉甸甸的箱子像是拿着气球。

我感到我是一群人。
在面店吃面的时候他们就在我的面前
围桌而坐。他们尖脸和方脸，哈哈大笑，他们有一点儿会计的
假正经。但是我饿极了。他们哼着旧电影的插曲，
跨入我的碗里。

我感到我是一群人。
但是他们聚成了一堆恐惧。我上公交车，
车就摇晃。进一个酒吧，里面停电。我只好步行
去虹口、外滩、广场，绕道回家。
我感到我的脚里有另外一双脚。

1997，6，10

一次抵制

当几个车站扮演了几个省份，
大地好像寂寞的果皮，某种酝酿，
你经过更好的冒充，一些忍耐，
迎接的仅仅是英俊的假设。

经过提速，我来得早了，
还是不够匹配你的依然先进，依然突兀，
甚至决断，反而纵容了我的加倍的迟钝。

They flowed out like beads of sweat. They were squatting, jumping,
Blocking me from moving forward. They wore watches and flowery
    shirts,
And they carried heavy suitcases as if they were balloons.

I felt I was a multitude.
Eating noodles at the noodle shop they were right in front of me,
They sat down around a table. Some had pointy faces, some square
    faces, laughing, they looked like accountants
With feigned solemnity. I was famished. They hummed musical scores
    from old movies,
Stepping into my bowl.

I felt I was a multitude.
But they gathered into a heap of fear. I boarded the transit bus,
And the bus shook. I entered a bar, the electricity went out. All I could
    do was
Walk to Hongkou, to the Bund, to People's Square, the roundabout
    way home.
I felt in my feet there was another pair of feet.

10 June 1997

A ONE-TIME RESISTANCE

When a few train stations impersonate a few provinces
And the land is like a lonely fruit peel, something stirring inside,
After your enhanced duplicity, you exercise some patience,
What you greet is merely the hypothesis of handsomeness.

Having sped up, I've arrived early,
There's still no way to match your customary sophistication, your
    customary dignity,
Your resolve, and yet you indulge my redoubled torpidity.

这果核般的地点也是从车窗扔下，
像草率、误解、易于忽略的装置，
不够酸楚，但可以期待。
因为必须的未来是公式挥泪。

我知道，一切意外都源于各就各位，
任何周密，任何疏漏，都是匠心越轨，
不过，操纵不如窥视，局部依靠阻止。

2005，11，18，车过山东的时候

This place is like a fruit pit tossed out the car window,
Like carelessness, misunderstanding, an easily neglected installation.
I'm not miserable enough, but I'm still expectant.
Because the inevitable future is your perfunctory shedding of tears.

I know, all things unexpected originate in each maintaining one's
        position,
Any meticulousness, any oversight is an ingenious transgression,
But a furtive glance outdoes manipulation, and partially relies on
        obstruction.

                    18 November 2005, while passing through Shandong

横渡伶仃洋

对历史无知者横渡现实之伶仃洋
会使你晕船，在教科书以外
船尾的飞沫像白孔雀尾巴盛开
曹辉的午饭在他的腹中剧烈地翻滚
而一片白色的药片使我的心平静
中间状态的人在舱内昏睡
马达均匀的轰鸣外套古老的涛声
我们的船抚摸着伶仃洋、切开了伶仃洋
浸入其中，漫溢出的海水将两岸淹没
从荒凉的海上驶向未来的城
蛇口的楼影像朝阳升起

从珠海到深圳
液体、柔软的路和移动的坟
有时候我们停在它的中间
不离一个地方更远或者更近
我们扩展了它但无法结束它

Han Dong

Han Dong, born in Nanjing in 1961, entered Shandong University in 1978. He began working in Xi'an upon graduation, but in 1984 returned to Nanjing where he now lives and works. A full-time writer since 1993, he is well known for his poetry, novels, essays, and blog posts. He was a leading light in the 1998 "Fracture" movement and has edited websites and literary magazines such as *Them* and *Today*. He has published four novels, one of which was long-listed for the Man Asian Literary Prize in 2008, and has won several independent poetry prizes.

Translated by Nicky Harman

CROSSING THE LINGDINGYANG, THE LONELY SEA

For those ignorant of history, crossing the real-life Lonely Sea
Can make you seasick, outside of textbooks
At the stern, flying foam blooms like a peacock's tail
Cao Hui's lunch lurches violently in his belly
While a white pill calms me down
Those in a middling state doze in the cabin
The engine's steady roar cloaks the ancient lapping of waves
Our boat is stroking the Lonely Sea, cuts it open
Becomes immersed in it, the brimming waters swamp both shores
From the desolate sea it sails to the coming city
The image of Shekou's buildings rises up like the morning sun

From Zhuhai to Shenzhen
A fluid, supple road and mobile tomb
Sometimes we stop in the middle of it
Not farther from one place or nearer
We've expanded it but are unable to end it

在鱼和水兽的家里
并无礼地立于那里的屋顶
我想到了死，但不是认真的
我的思想更倾向于两小时以后的宴会
所有晕眩的印象都将被抹掉
只留下"丁零"洋敲击着碗盏

此外，我记得特殊环境中与
张文娟小姐唯一的私人接触——
给了她一枚白色的药片
但不是递与床头我妻子避孕的那枚
（"避晕"而非"避孕"）
她接过，咽得也勉强
因为她的胃正呼应着伶仃洋
不像我那么敏感，但有
更值得纠正的痛苦表情
她的红西服也蒙尘、起皱
并手握相当粗的铁管栏杆进入了底舱
哈，白茫茫的伶仃洋也不是爱情的海洋！

1994

小姐

她的衣服从来不换。
我注意到，它是美丽的、肮脏的，
它是表姐的。
穷人无二件。

我注意到她身处的店堂、我们分属的阶级，
而性的微尘无理智地来往。
裸体的必要，比穿衣打扮更简单。
服饰比身体更令人羞愧，是可能的。

And at the home of fish and water beasts
We stand rudely on their roofs
I've thought of dying, but not seriously
My thoughts lean more toward the banquet in two hours' time
Then, all impressions of queasiness will be erased
Leaving only the ding-a-ling sea knocking against the dishes

That aside, I remember the special circumstances in which
I had my only private contact with Miss Zhang Wenjuan
I gave her a white pill
Not the contraceptive pill I passed to my wife in bed
(An anti-seasick pill, not "the" pill)
She took it, forced herself to swallow
For her stomach, which heaved along with the Lonely Sea
She seemed less sensitive than me, but wore
A pained expression much more in need of righting
Her red suit was dusty and crumpled
And then she gripped the crude iron handrail and went below to
         the cabin
Ha! The white expanse of the Lonely Sea is not the ocean of love!

1994

WAITRESS

She's never changed her clothes.
I notice they're pretty, and dirty.
They belong to her cousin,
The poor don't have a change of clothes.

I notice the shop she's in, our class difference,
Dust specks of sex, irrational, move between us.
The need for nakedness, much simpler than dressing up.
A fine outfit is far more shaming than a body, possibly.

"小姐，你的穷
是空缺的财富。
你的空虚很实在，脸蛋儿被油腻衬托得更美。"

她的青春在搬动桌椅中度过一年。

1995

无题

黑暗太深，如双目紧闭
如挖去眼球
寂静使耳轮萎缩
既如此
手脚又有何用？

一块顽石之内
思如奔马
方寸之地
冲撞不得出

就把封闭的这团献给你吧
使劲地抛出去
击中一条母狗

或永不落地
一颗星星发出自己看不见但照耀山川的
无聊的光辉

2003

"Miss, your poverty
Is a wealth of vacancy.
Your emptiness quite material, your face made lovelier by contrast with
        the grease."

A year of her youth has passed in moving chairs and tables.

1995

UNTITLED

This darkness is too deep, like eyes tightly shut
Like eyeballs dug out
The stillness makes the ear rims shrivel
This being so
What use are hands and feet?

Inside a hard rock
Thoughts gallop
Cannot break out
From this cramped space.

Here, let me give this sealed-up chunk to you
Flung violently away
It strikes a bitch dog

Or never falls to earth
A star gives light it cannot see itself but shines on hills and rivers—
A meaningless brilliance.

2003

买回一本有关六朝文人的书

从城市坡道上步行回家
我的手触摸到松树树梢
在寒冷的夜晚树梢会
弯曲，成为黑暗
让星辰照耀

不必俯身，我可以看清楚石头的居所
河流在暗影里像一柄斧子

我经过天文台的半圆形山丘
迎面进入了冬天的太阳
稽康飞翔的身姿
左思对刺客的吟咏
他们的悲凉远胜于我

澄澈的中午也看见星辰
人死了多年
水依旧明亮

1986

Chen Dongdong

Chen Dongdong, born in 1961 in Shanghai, is a graduate of Shanghai Normal University's Department of Chinese. His writing career began in 1980, when, as a member of contemporary poetry circles, he edited a series of literary magazines: *Zuopin, Qingxiang,* and *Nanfang shizhi.* His own poetry is collected in a number of volumes.

Translated by Andrea Lingenfelter

BRINGING HOME A NEW BOOK ABOUT SIX DYNASTIES LITERATI

Walking home along a sloping city road
my hands grazing the branch tips of pines
On cold nights those tips might
furl, turning into darkness
making constellations blaze

Without bending down, I can see where stones dwell
The deeply shaded river like an ax

Passing by the half-circular mound of the observatory
leads straight into the winter sun
Ji Kang's body in flight
Zuo Si's ode to the assassin
Their anguish far surpassed my own

I can see the stars even in the crystal brilliance of midday
Those men have been dead for so many years
And the waters still shine as bright as before

1986

病中

病中一座花园，香樟高于古柏
忧郁的护士仿佛天鹅
从水到桥，从浓荫到禁药
在午睡的氛围里梦见了飞翔
——那滞留的太阳
已经为八月安排下大雨

一个重要的老人呻吟
惊动指甲鲜红的情人：抚慰
清洗、扪弄和注射
他陈旧的眼眶滚出泪水
抵挡玫瑰和金钱的疼痛

隔开廊道，我身凭长窗
我低俯这医院里酷暑的风景
阴云四合，池鱼们上升
得病的妇女等待着浇淋
当我的视线自花园移开
第一滴雨
落进了第一个死者的掌心

1990

DURING AN ILLNESS

During an illness, a garden, camphor trees taller than ancient cypresses
Mournful nurses drifting like swans
from water to bridge, from deep shade to forbidden drugs
dreaming of flight in the haze of a midday nap
Bogged down, the sun
has arranged heavy rains for August

An elderly VIP is moaning
startling his crimson-nailed lover: consoling
cleansing, stroking and injecting
The worn orbits of his eye sockets leak tears
insulating him from the pain of roses and money

Across the hallway, I lean against a tall window
looking down on the hospital's cruel summer landscape
Clouds close in on all sides, fish surface in the pond
ailing women await a sprinkling of water
When my gaze moves away from the garden
the first drop of rain
falls into the palm of the first one to die

1990

春秋来信

1

这个时辰的背面，才是我的家，
它在另一个城市里挂起了白旗。
天还没亮，睡眠的闸门放出几辆
载重卡车，它们恐龙般在拐口
撕抢某件东西，本就没有的东西。
我醒来。
　　　　身上一颗绿扣子滚落。

2

我们的绿扣子，永恒的小赘物。
云朵，砌建着上海。
　　　　　我心中一幅蓝图
正等着增砖添瓦。我挪向亮处，
那儿，鹤，闪现了一下。你的信
立在室中央一柱阳光中理着羽毛——
是的，无需特赦。得从小白菜里，
从豌豆苗和冬瓜，找出那一个理解来，

Zhang Zao

Zhang Zao, born in 1962, received a PhD from Tübingen University. A prominent representative of contemporary Chinese poetry, he spent many years in the West and was a scholar and teacher of Chinese poetry and world literature. Proficient in English, German, French, and Russian, he has translated Rilke, Celan, Heine, Char, and other poets. He resided in Beijing, where he was a professor in the College of Literature and Broadcasting at Central University for Nationalities until his death in 2010.

Translated by Nick Kaldis

A YEAR OF LETTERS

1

It's the obverse of this moment, which is in fact my home,
in some other city it raises a white flag.
Not yet daybreak, slumber's floodgates release a handful of
leaden trucks, like dinosaurs they round the corner
clawing for a certain something, a certain something that isn't.
I awaken.
   A green button rolls from my body.

2

Our green button, eternal tiny superfluity.
Clouds, bricking Shanghai.
   A blueprint in my heart
awaits more brick and tile. I shift toward a bright spot,
there, a crane flares up for an instant. Your letters
stand in a column of sunbeams in the middle of the room, preening—
that's right, no need for amnesty. It must be from inside bok choy,
from pea shoots and winter melon, that understanding comes,

来关掉肥胖和机器——
　　　　　我深深地
被你身上的矛盾吸引，移到窗前。
四月如此清澈，好似烈酒的反光，
街景颤抖着组合成深奥的比例。
是的，我喊不醒现实。而你的声音
追上我的目力所及："我，

就是你呀！我也漂在这个时辰里。
工地上就要爆破了，我在我这边
鸣这面锣示警。游过来呀，
接住这面锣，它就是你错过了的一切。"

　　　　　3
我拾起地上的绿扣子，吹了吹。
开始忙我的事儿。
　　　　　静的时候，
窗下经过的邮差以为我是我的肖像；
有时我趴在桌面昏昏欲睡，
双手伸进空间，像伸进一副镣铐，

哪儿，哪儿，是我们的精确呀？
　　　　　　......　绿扣子。

　　　　　　　　　　　　　　　　1997

告别孤独堡

　　　　1
上午，仿佛有一种樱桃之远；　有
一杯凉水在口中微微发甜，
使人竟置身到他自身之外
电话铃响了三下，又杳然中断，
会是谁呢？

come switch off obesity and machines—
    I'm deeply
drawn by the contradictions on your body, moved over to the window.
Such a limpid April, like the play of light on liquor,
shuddering street scenes congeal into abstruse proportions.
That's right, my cries can't awaken reality. But your voice
follows to the furthest reaches of my eyes: "I,

am you! I'm adrift in this moment too.
At the construction site it's demolition time; I'm over here
sounding the siren gong. Swim over here!
grab hold of this gong, it's all that you've passed up."

    3
I pick up the green button, blow on it.
Start tending to my own affairs.
    In the silence,
the mailman passing beneath the window takes me for my portrait;
sometimes I drowsily sprawl across the tabletop,
both hands reaching into the air, like reaching into a pair of handcuffs,

where, where, rests our exactitude?
    ...a green button.

1997

FAREWELL (TO THE) FORTRESS OF SOLITUDE

    1
Morning, seems like some kind of cherry span; a
cool glass of water turns faintly sweet on the tongue,
unexpectedly at some remove from himself
the phone rings three times, then abrupt silence,
who could it be?

我忽然记起两天前回这儿的夜路上，
我设想去电话亭给我的空房间拨电话：
假如真的我听到我在那边
对我说："Hello?"
我的惊恐，是否会一窝蜂地钻进听筒？

2

你没有来电话，而我
两小时之后又将分身异地。
秋天正把它的帽子收进山那边的箱子里。
燕子，给言路铺着电缆，仿佛
有一种羁绊最终能被俯瞰……

3

有一种怎样的渺不可见
泄露在窗台上，袖子边：
有一种抵抗之力，用打火机
对空旷派出一只狐狸，那

颉颃的瞬翼
使森林边一台割草机猛省地跪向静寂，

使睡衣在衣架上鼓起胸肌，它
登上预感
如登上去市中心的班车。

4

是呀，我们约好去沙漠，它是
绿的妆镜，那儿，你会给它
带来唯一的口红，纸和卫生品；
但去那儿，我们得先等候在机场的咖啡亭。
是呀，樱桃多远。而咖啡，仿佛
知道你不会来而使过客颤抖。

I suddenly recall (that) two nights ago on the way back here,
I imagined going to a phone booth to dial up my empty room:
if I'd really heard myself on the other end
saying: "Hello?"
my trepidation, could it swarm into the receiver?

2

You never called, and I
two hours later will again be in another place.
Autumn is storing its hat in the chest on that side of the mountain.
Swallows, laying cable for administrative channels, seems like
some kind of yoke can finally be looked down at...

3

There's some kind of somehow so faintly
divulging on a sill, by the sleeves:
there's some kind of resistance, using a cigarette lighter
dispatches a fox into the vastness, those

haughty blinking wings
cause a lawnmower at forest's edge to kneel in epiphany toward silence,

causing the pajamas on the hanger to puff up their pecs, and
embark on a premonition
like boarding the downtown bus.

4

Yup, we had arranged to visit the desert, it's
a green makeup mirror, there, you'll bring it
only lipstick, paper tissue, and sanitary products:
but to get there, we'll have to first wait in the airport coffee kiosk.
Yup, cherries so distant. But coffee, seems like
it knows you're not coming and it makes the passersby shudder.

咖啡推开一个纹身的幻象，空间弯曲，而
有一种对称，
命令左中指冲刺般翘起：

"决不给纳粹半点机会！"

2003

Coffee shoves away a tattooed phantasm, space is warped, yet
there's some kind of symmetry,
ordering the left middle finger to snap to attention:

"Never give an inch to the Nazis!"

2003

孔子

我的生命中只有两件事，出生和灭亡。
我不曾唱过那支辱没我的歌：
泰山就要倒了，房梁就要塌了，哲人就要死了。
我说过下面的话，舌头老掉了牙：

因为空气中没有仁爱，我要求仁爱。
因为大地上没有忠诚，我要求忠诚。
因为人心中没有惧怕，我要求惧怕。
因为我终将一死，所以我指鹿为马。

多少人用我的头脑思想
我的头脑却空空荡荡。
我的教育完全失败。
我的学生只配做塾师。

而我的诗歌只剩下了偏旁。
我的名声只剩下了羞耻。

Qing Ping

Qing Ping, pen name of Qingping Wang, was born in Suzhou, Jiangsu Province, in March 1962. He enrolled at Peking University in 1983 and has remained in the capital for work up to the present day. He began writing in the eighties, was awarded the Liu Li-an Poetry Prize in 1996, and published his first collection in 2007. His works have been widely published in collections such as *Chinese Poetry Critique* and *Another Kind of Nation: An Anthology of Contemporary Chinese Poetry*, as well as in online venues such as the Forum for Literary Freedom.

Translated by Lucas Klein

CONFUCIUS

There are just two things in my life, birth and demise.
I never sang that song that disgraced me:
Mount Tai's going to topple, the roof beams're gonna fall, the
      philosopher's about to die.
This is what I said, with my tongue losing my teeth:

Because there is no humanity in the air, I ask for humanity.
Because there is no loyalty on the earth, I ask for loyalty.
Because there is no fear in our hearts, I ask for fear.
Because in the end I will die, I bear false witness.

How many people use my brain to think
While my brain is just plain empty.
My education has been a total failure.
My students are only fit to be tutors.

My poems leave extra letters.
My reputation leaves only shame.

我的灭亡只剩下了棺材。
我的棺材只剩下了木板。

但是，谁在鲁国的乡间小道上看到过我的身影？
谁享用过我亲手腌制的腊肉？
谁，在一次私人谈话中小偷般记下了
那些完全不属于我的可怕的言辞？

我知晓大多数不可靠的事物。我懂得遗忘。
我写出了它们：一两个年龄。
寒冷的冬夜我偶然梦醒
听到的只有一个声音——

风的呼啸，风的生长，风的灭亡。
当我听到万籁俱寂唯余风的声音
我的儿子便是姜子牙或伍子胥
虞舜或纣王，周公或仲尼。

我写下了"逝者如斯夫，不舍昼夜"。
我写下了乌托邦——一个旧魂灵。
我命中注定也写下了历史：我的三千弟子
七十二种黑暗，七十二道鬼影。

1997

阴天写下的一首诗

天阴得像一块抹布。
那么恶俗的一句话闪现在头脑中。
远方，又有人枉死于一个国家的断代史。
身边的乌云，仿佛不在头顶，
而在人民兴奋得沙哑的街头檄文。

My death leaves only a coffin.
My coffin leaves only plywood.

But who has seen my shadow in the backwoods of Lu?
Who has enjoyed the salt pork I cured with my own hands?
Who, like a thief, recorded from a private conversation
Those fearsome sayings that aren't even mine?

I comprehend most unreliable things. I know what it is to forget.
I write them out: an age or two.
On wintry nights I might wake from a dream
Hearing only one sound—

The howl of the wind, the growth of the wind, the demise of the wind.
When a myriad noises fall silent only the sound of wind remains.
My son is either Jiang Ziya or Wu Zixu,
The Emperor or the Usurper, the Duke of Zhou or Confucius.

I wrote, "The river passeth on thusly, unceasing be it day or night."
I wrote Utopia—an old departed soul.
In my life I was destined to write history: my three thousand disciples,
Seventy-two kinds of darkness, seventy-two types of ghost.

1997

A POEM WRITTEN ON AN OVERCAST DAY

The sky darkens like a rag.
That vulgar line flashes in my head.
Far away in some nation's dynastic history, someone else dies for
      no reason.
Ominous clouds at my side, it's like they're not above me
but are on the street denouncing the enemy in the people's hoarse
      excitement.

一下午都像倒空的米袋，鼓不起半点劲。
天上有什么？我先给自己加一个罪名：冰。
因为我的答案太冷酷：天上有的是
一两天之后的万里无云。
在我周围，越来越多的书仿佛很卑鄙地后退，
而不离开它们的期待。
我恼火么？是的。但我又不能将它们销毁。
对于我，它们才是这幢半个多世纪的大楼里
经久不散的阴霾。
我终于想到，我不是一个好人。
在道德里滚了几十年，原来只是道德的一个小化身。
我推开窗，看着飞驰而过的运钞车，
心想，管他呢。我的祖国不值得批评。

2009，2，23

写给我的一首诗

在广阔的昔日，多少人
凭着狭隘获取菲薄的名声。
地球上，只有宇宙是平均。
它的意义，近乎一篇唐朝的檄义。

和无限多的名字连在一起
没有想象中那样的丧失。
我的容貌也不是唯一。我的性情
曾令我骄傲——当我还不了解另一些否定。

岁月的火箭只在云海里穿行。
回头看，白发的苗圃和命运之船
无不来自我多疑的铅笔。
上溯十年，我不会揭穿那么多比喻。

The whole afternoon's like an emptied sack of rice, unable to puff
     itself up.
What's there in the sky? First let me give myself an indictment: ice.
Because my answer is too cold: what's in the sky is
ten thousand miles of cloudlessness, in a day or two.
Around me, more and more books seem to be retreating in depravity,
yet they can't leave behind their anticipations.
Does it annoy me? Yes. But then again I can't burn them.
To me, they're the real haze that won't disperse
inside this fifty-some-year-old building.
Finally I've got it, I'm not a good person.
Rolling around in morality for decades, in the end I'm just one of
     morality's bit incarnations.
I push open the window, watching the armored vehicles fly by.
I think, Hell with 'em. My country isn't even worth my criticism.

                                                           23 February 2009

A POEM WRITTEN FOR MYSELF

In the vastness of yesterday, how many people
have acquired renown out of narrowness.
In this world, only the universe is equitable.
In its meaning, it approaches a Tang dynasty declaration of war.

Being connected with a limitless number of names
is not as deprived as it's imagined to be.
Nor is my appearance unique. My disposition
once made me arrogant—when I didn't know of other negations.

The rockets of age only traverse the *mare nubium*.
Looking back, the white-hair nursery and the ship of fate
both emanate from my skeptical pencil.
Retracing the decade, I wouldn't expose so many metaphors.

但，童年确乎不可信。
我曾望见奥古斯丁转圈的人生
迷惑过纯正的中国母亲。
她们嗜好战争的孩子，半辈子都在回忆里射击。

不停的废弃，未尝构成我的遗憾。
人和一个人的融合，离别于革命的天然。
四十七年过去，我看到波浪的准确。
而更早，我在爱情中已无视了一切。

2009，3，13

But youth is indeed beyond credibility.
I have gazed upon the revolving life of Augustine
and baffled pure Chinese mothers.
Their children are addicted to war—half their lives are gunfire in
      memories.

Endless discard has not constituted my regret.
The coalescence of person and person, taking leave of the nature of
      revolution.
Forty-seven years have gone by, and I see the precision of waves.
Whereas earlier, out of love I disregarded it all.

13 March 2009

废灯泡

灯丝断了，它从光明的位置退休
它最后的一眨眼解除高烧
回到寒冷而透明的废品博物馆
我记得孩子是怎样处理废灯泡的
"啪"的一声，听个响儿
宁为玉碎，不求瓦全
灯的死法如此悲壮
除此之外，灯还有什么用？
象征，对；模仿，对
它是从生产线下来的太阳的模型
它饱满的真空形成小宇宙
发明家爱迪生对它情有独钟
光和玻璃是乌托邦的建筑
在每一家庭的理想国里
人只是一个快乐的囚徒
灯泡废弃的大脑依然可爱
如果你家有孩子千万不要存废灯泡
它物质的属性易碎、扎手

Sen Zi

Sen Zi was born in Hulan County, Heilongjiang Province, in 1962. In 1987 he graduated from the Department of Art at Zhoukou Normal University, Henan. He has been a soldier and a teacher and has published collections of both poetry and essays. He edited nine issues of the poetry magazine *Battlefront* and works for a newspaper where he resides, in Pingdingshan, Henan Province.

Translated by Alice Xin Liu

BURNED-OUT BULBS

The filaments are broken, they retire from positions of light
Its last blink has relieved its high fever
Returning itself to the cold yet transparent Museum of Waste
I remember how children treated burned-out bulbs
To hear a "pop," the sound it makes
Better to die gloriously like a piece of jade than to live dully
The death of a bulb is so solemn and stirring
What other uses does a bulb have?
Symbolism, yes; imitation, yes
It's a model of the sun from a production line
Its full-bellied vacuum forms a small universe
Edison the inventor had special affection for it
Light and glass are the architects of Utopia
In the Republic of every home
Humans are mere happy prisoners
A brain abandoned by bulbs is still lovely
If you have children, don't ever keep burned-out bulbs
Fragility, hand-prickling are their properties

因此，对一只废灯泡执行死刑是必然的
就像我们不断埋葬昨天的理想
还会有别的光线照进肉体的角落
还会有灯的嫡孙守着空缺
真是这样，确实是这样
两年前，城里的灯泡厂关闭了
厂区地皮卖给房地产开发商
生产线上的女工被安置到医药商店
调侃的人也许会说：现在
我们需要的是药，不是光

1997，3，25

烧树叶

烧树叶，一个国家头痛
它需要一根火柴或一根银针

我许久没有看到街头的火
我早已忘记篝火旁的野人

发愣的眼睛，因看而空洞
空洞的心或物质的稻草人

确认：紧张中的走神儿
我太大意了，将自己混同于

气味、烟雾，混同于困倦
和恶心，我从来不知道

树上的鸟巢、蚂蚁们的建设
原则和方针，我出门和进门

Therefore, it's necessary to put a burned-out bulb to death
Just the way we continuously bury yesterday's ideals
There will still be other light to shine into the corners of the body
There will still be descendants waiting to take its place
It really is so, it truly is
Two years ago, the lightbulb factory in town was shut down
The factory land sold to real estate developers
The production line's female workers were sent to the pharmacy
People who like to banter might say: Now
What we need is medicine, not light

25 March 1997

BURNING LEAVES

Burning leaves, a national headache
Only a matchstick or a silver needle is needed

I haven't seen street fire for a long time
I forgot long ago the savages near the bonfire

Eyes in a daze, they are hollow from looking
A hollow heart or a simply made scarecrow

Confirmation: distraction due to nerves
I was too careless, mixing myself with

Smell, smoke, mixing with sleepiness
And nausea, I never knew

Bird's nest in a tree, ants' construction
Principles and guidelines, I exit and enter

听和看，报纸的蝙蝠飞乱
下午和黄昏。从我的耳朵里

扯出电话线，嘴唇上测量
谎话的温度，我是我自己的

蔬菜市场、银行、电影院，我是
也可以什么都不是，落叶或情人

看微暗的火裹住树叶舞蹈
我只能是身处灰土中的人

或者是某物，引火烧身
当秋天低过我的额头，留下疤痕

1997，11，7

夜宿山中

夜色抹去几个山头，登山的路像两小时前的
晾衣绳已模糊不清，我们饮酒、聊天
不知不觉，夜已深更。乡村饭店跛脚的老板娘
烧好一壶开水，等着我们洗脸洗脚
她还铺好被褥，补好了枕套
星星大如牛斗，明亮得让人畏惧、吃惊
仿佛有一双银色的弹簧手，伸出来要将
我劫走。多少年了，我以为这种原始的宗教
感情不存在了，今夜它活生生地扯动我
没有润滑油的脖颈，向上，拉动，
千百只萤火虫、蝙蝠、飞蛾扑入我怀中
我耳边回响蜜蜂蜇过一般的低语
"头顶的星空，内心的道德律。"大学毕业时

Watching and listening, newspaper bats are fluttering around
Afternoon and dusk. From inside my ears

Tear out telephone cords, and measure with my lips
The temperature of the lies, I am my own

Vegetable market, bank, cinema, I am
I could also be nothing, fallen leaves or lovers

Looking at the dim fire wrap the leaves in dance
I can only be someone whose body is in dust

Or a certain something else, I was playing with fire
When autumn is lower than my forehead, a scar is left

7 November 1997

STAYING OVERNIGHT ON A MOUNTAIN

The dusk erased a few mountaintops, a two-hour road up
The clothesline became hazy, we drank and talked
Night fell and we didn't know. A lame-legged village restaurant owner
Boiled a pot of hot water for washing our faces and feet
She made the bed, too, and mended the pillowcases
The stars were big as constellations, scary and shockingly bright
Like a pair of silver-springed hands, extended out to
Take me away. For many years, I thought this kind of primitive religious
Emotion had ceased to exist, but it excitedly pulled me toward it
An ungreased neck, pulling, upward
Hundreds and thousands of fireflies, bats, and moths rush into my arms
Echoes near my ears are whispers that were stung by bees
"The starry sky above and the moral law within me." When I graduated
    from college

我把它抄在一位好友的留言本上，星空和道德
也舍我而去。这几年，我在陋室里和影子争论
终极价值和意义，却没有跳出紧闭的窗口
呼吸一下夜空的芳香。一位女散文家
曾同我聊过她去高原的感受，"夜里，月亮
大得吓人，我一夜不敢睡觉……"
此刻，我似乎明白，或者是愈加糊涂了
童年蒙昧中敬畏的事物，不是没有缘由
或许，我出生前曾在月亮或火星的陨石坑里睡过觉
更坏的说法是我被洗过脑，像传说中的
玛丽莲·梦露在澳洲成了牧羊人的妻子
今夜，我感到自己似乎犯下了"重生罪"
覆盖，一代覆盖一代。我自以为清醒地在
楼顶间写下过这样的诗句：
"城市的浮光掠影惊吓了胆小的星星。"
现在看来那完全是胡扯，自欺欺人，
我抬头寻找着银河，在乡村饭店前的小河边坐下
脑海里忽然冒出一句话"宇宙诞生于大爆炸"。

1999，4，15

I copied this into a friend's notebook, the stars and morality
Have already left me. These years, in my humble room I debate with
    my shadow
The ultimate meaning and value, but I didn't jump out the tightly
    shut window
To breathe the fragrance of the night sky. One woman essayist
Discussed with me her feelings about the plateau: "At night, the moon
Was so big it was scary, all night I was too afraid to sleep…"
During those moments I almost understood, or was I more confused?
Things I was ignorantly in awe of as a child weren't without cause
Maybe, before I was born I slept in one of the craters on the moon or
    on Mars
I've been brainwashed, would be a worse explanation, like the
    legend where
Marilyn Monroe became a herder's wife in Australia
Tonight, I felt that I committed the "sin of rebirth"
One generation overlays the next. I thought that I was clearheaded when
I wrote this line of poetry in the garret:
"The fleetingness of the city scared the timid stars."
That seems like complete nonsense now, deceiving others and myself
I search for the Milky Way, I sit down by a stream near the village diner
This pops into my head: "The universe was born out of the Big Bang."

15 April 1999

母子图

在上班的巴士上，前面右边第一排
坐着一个高大、健康、英俊的少年，
他身边坐着一个三十多岁的女人，
显然是他母亲。他不时指点窗外的景物，
一边描述和评论。不是絮絮叨叨那种，
而是声音坚实，吐字清晰，听起来特别享受。
他母亲总是点点头，或低声回答，像情人一样。
她看上去非常普通，不惹眼，但因为她儿子的缘故，
你会愈看愈觉得她漂亮、美丽、迷人、性感，
她染了淡淡的赤色头发，一绺绺发丝
轻柔地散在颈上，一个大耳环偶尔摇晃一下。

Huang Canran

Huang Canran was born in a mountain village in Quanzhou, Fujian, in 1963. He immigrated to Hong Kong in 1978 and returned, to Guangzhou, to study journalism at Jinan University from 1984 to 1988. Since 1990 he has worked as an international news translator for *Da Gong Bao*. He has published several collections of both poetry and reviews. He regularly translates Western poetry and is Susan Sontag's primary Chinese translator.

Translated by Gerald Maa

A DRAWING OF MOTHER AND SON

On the bus headed to work, in the front-right row
sits a big, healthy, handsome teenager,
a thirtysomething woman sitting by his side,
obviously his mother. He often points at the scenery outside the window,
commenting and describing. Not the long-winded sort,
but rather with a firm voice, clearly enunciating, which sounds quite
    enjoyable.
His mother keeps on nodding, or answering in a low voice, the way a
    lover would.
She looks plain, not eye-catching, but because of her son,
the more you look, the more you will feel she's pretty, beautiful,
    enchanting, sexy,
hair she dyed to a hint of red, lock after lock
softly spreading on her neck, a large earring occasionally swaying.

母女图

那对母女坐在公园的长凳上谈心，
隔着一个空位。她们放松地靠着椅背的姿态，
她们闲闲地聊天的姿态
给了我这颗近来不胜忧烦的心多少的安慰，
虽然我知道，我知道，她们可能
非常可能是在互相安慰。

A DRAWING OF MOTHER AND DAUGHTER

That mother and daughter open up their hearts while sitting on a park
        bench,
separated by a vacant seat. Their relaxed posture leaning against the
        bench back,
their posture of idle chatter
gives much comfort to my troubled heart,
even though I know, I know, they likely
very likely are comforting each other.

蚊子志

一万只蚊子团结成一只老虎，减少至九千只团结成一只豹子，减少至八千只团结成一只走不动的黑猩猩。而一只蚊子就是一只蚊子。

一只吸血的蚊子，母蚊子，与水蛭、吸血鬼同归一类，还可加上吸血的官僚、地主、资本家。天下生物若按饮食习惯分类，可分为食肉者、食草者和吸血者。

在历史的缝隙间，到处是蚊子。它们见证乃至参与过砍头、车裂、黄河决堤、卖儿卖女，只是二十五部断代史中没有一节述及蚊子。

Xi Chuan

Xi Chuan, whose real name is Liu Jun, was born in 1963 and graduated from Peking University's Department of English in 1985. In 2002 he participated in the University of Iowa's International Writing Program, and in 2007 was a visiting professor at NYU. He currently teaches at the Beijing Central Art Academy. His many collections of poetry and essays have won prizes, domestic and international, and his translations, including essays by Borges, have been widely acclaimed. His writing has been translated into many languages.

Translated by Lucas Klein

NOTES ON THE MOSQUITO

Ten thousand mosquitoes unite into a tiger, reduced to nine thousand they unite into a leopard, reduced to eight thousand and they unite into an immobile chimpanzee. But one mosquito is just one mosquito.

The hemophagous mosquito, the female of the species, is in the same category as the leech and the vampire, to which could also be added the bloodsucking bureaucrat, the landlord, the capitalist. Were all creatures under heaven to be grouped according to diet, they would then be grouped into carnivorous, herbivorous, and hemophagous.

Mosquitoes are everywhere in the crevices of history. They have witnessed and even participated in beheadings, human quartering by horse-cart, busted embankments on the Yellow River, and the peddling of sons and daughters, yet the twenty-five books of the dynastic histories contain not one mention of the mosquito.

我们今天撞上的蚊子，其祖先可追溯至女娲的时代。（女娲，美女也，至少《封神演义》中有此一说。女娲性喜蚊子，但《封神演义》中无此一说。）

但一只蚊子的寿限，几乎在一个日出与日落之间，或两个日出与日落之间，因此一只蚊子生平平均可见到四五个人或二三十口猪或一匹马。这意味着蚊子从未建立起有关善恶的观念。

有人不开窗，不开门，害怕进蚊子，他其实是被蚊子所拘禁。有人不得不上街头的厕所，当他被蚊子叮咬，他发现虽奇痒但似乎尚可容忍。

我来到世上的目的之一，便是被蚊子叮咬。它们在我的皮肤上扎进针管，它们在我的影子里相约纳凉，它们在我有毒的呼吸里昏死过去。

深夜，一个躺在床上半睡半醒的人自打耳光。他不是在反省，而是听见了蚊子的嗡嗡声。他的力量用得越大，他打死蚊子的机率越高，听起来他的自责越严厉。

那么蚊子死后变成谁？一个在我面前嗡嗡乱飞的人，他的前世必是一只蚊子。有些小女孩生得过于瘦小，我们通常也称她们为"蚊子"。

The mosquito we run into today could trace its ancestry back to the era when Nüwa repaired the heavens. (Nüwa was a beauty, or so is told in *The Investiture of the Gods*. Nüwa's nature was to delight in mosquitoes, though such is not told in *The Investiture of the Gods*.)

Yet the longevity of a mosquito is fixed nearly between sunup and sundown, or between two sunups and sundowns, and therefore in the whole life of a mosquito it might only meet an average of four or five people or twenty or thirty pigs or one horse. This suggests that mosquitoes never establish viewpoints on good and evil.

Some people do not open windows, do not open doors, for fear that mosquitoes will come in, but in fact they are being imprisoned by mosquitoes. Some people have no choice but to use public toilets on the street, and when they are bitten by mosquitoes, they discover that the severity of its itch is nevertheless tolerable.

Of my goals in being on this earth, one is to be bitten by a mosquito. They pierce their needles into my skin, they convene to cool off in my shade, they expire in the poison of my breath.

In the depths of the night, someone half asleep in bed slaps himself. He is not being introspective, rather he has heard the buzz of a mosquito. The greater his force, the greater his success rate in killing mosquitoes, the sterner the sounds of his self-reproach.

So who does the mosquito turn into after it dies? Someone buzzing and flitting in front of me, he must have been a mosquito in a previous life. Some girls are born way too skinny, and we usually call them "mosquitoes."

保护大自然，就是保护蚊子及其他，其中包括疟疾之神。保护大自然，同时加快清凉油制造业。就是努力将蚊子驱赶出大自然。但事实证明这极其困难。

把蚊子带上飞机，带上火车，带往异国他乡，能够加深我们的思乡之情，增强我们对于大地的认同感。每一次打开行李箱，都会飞出一只蚊子。

蚊子落过和蚊子不曾落过的地方，看上去没有区别，就像小偷摸过和小偷不曾摸过的地方，看上去也没有区别。细察小偷的行迹，放大镜里看见一只死去的蚊子。

2003，1

思想练习

尼采说"重估一切价值"，那就让我们重估这一把牙刷的价值吧。牙刷也许不是牙刷？或牙刷也许并不仅仅是牙刷？如果我们拒绝重估牙刷的价值，我们就是重估了尼采的价值。

尼采思想，这让我们思想时有点恬不知耻。但难道我们不是在恬不知耻地模仿鸟雀歌唱，恬不知耻地模仿白云沉默？难道我们不是在恬不知耻地恬不知耻？

To conserve nature is to conserve mosquitoes and others, which includes the god of malaria. To conserve nature, we must also accelerate our production of cooling balms. Then the mosquito can be vigorously driven from nature. Yet reality proves this to be highly difficult.

Bringing mosquitoes on an airplane, on a train, to other lands and foreign countries, can deepen our sensation of homesickness, and strengthen our identification with the earth. With each opening of a suitcase, a mosquito will fly out.

No one can tell the difference between a place where a mosquito has landed and a place where a mosquito has not landed, just as no one can tell the difference between places a thief has touched and places a thief has not touched. To scrutinize the trail of a thief is to see a dead mosquito under the microscope.

January 2003

EXERCISES IN THOUGHT

Nietzsche said, "Reevaluate all values," so in that case let's reevaluate the value of this toothbrush. Perhaps the toothbrush isn't a toothbrush? Or perhaps the toothbrush isn't simply a toothbrush? If we refuse to reevaluate the value of a toothbrush, we are reevaluating the value of Nietzsche.

Nietzschean thought, when we are in thought, makes us brazen and shameless. But does that mean that we aren't brazenly and shamelessly mimicking the singing of the sparrow, brazenly and shamelessly mimicking the silence of white clouds? Does that mean that we aren't brazenly and shamelessly being brazen and shameless?

有时即使我们想不出个所以然，我们也假装思想，就像一只苍蝇从一个字爬到另一个字，假装能够读懂一首诗。许多人假装思想，这说明思想是一件美丽的事。

但秃子不需要梳子，老虎不需要兵器，傻瓜不需要思想。一个无所需要的人几乎是一个圣人，但圣人也需要去数一数铁桥上巨大的铆钉用以消遣。这是圣人与傻瓜的区别。

尼采说一个人必须每天发现二十四条真理才能睡个好觉。但首先，一个人不应该发现那么多真理，以免真理在这世上供大于求；其次，一个人发现那么多真理就别想睡觉。

所以我敢肯定，尼采是一个从未睡过觉的人；或即使他睡着了，他也是在梦游。一个梦游者从不会遇上另一个梦游者。尼采从未遇到过上帝，所以他宣告"上帝死了"。

那么尼采遇到过王国维吗？没有。遇到过鲁迅吗？没有。遇到过我这个恬不知耻的人吗？也没有。所以尼采这个人或许并不存在，就像"灵魂"这个词或许并无所指。

思想有如飞翔，而飞翔令人晕眩，这是我有时不愿意思想的原因。思想有如恶习，而恶习让人体会到生活的有滋有味，这是我有时愿意思想的原因。

At times even if we can't figure out the whithers and wherefores, we still pretend to be in thought, like a fly crawling from one word to another, pretending to understand a poem. Many people pretend to be in thought, which proves that thought is a beautiful thing.

But the bald man doesn't need a comb, the tiger doesn't need weapons, the fool doesn't need thought. The person with no needs is practically a sage, but the sage also needs to go and count great big rivets on an iron bridge as a diversion. This is the difference between the sage and the fool.

Nietzsche said that a person must discover twenty-four truths each day before he can have a good night's sleep. But first of all, a person shouldn't find that many truths, so as not to let the supply of truths in this world exceed demand; secondly, anyone who discovers that many truths would hardly be able to fall asleep at all.

So I guarantee you, Nietzsche never slept; or if he did fall asleep, he was a sleepwalker. A sleepwalker will never meet another sleepwalker. Nietzsche never met God, which is why he declaimed, "God is dead."

But did Nietzsche ever meet Wang Guowei? No. Did he meet Lu Xun? No. Did he ever meet brazen and shameless me? Still no. So perhaps this Nietzsche never existed after all, just as the word *spirit* may mean nothing whatsoever.

Thought is like flying, though flying gives you vertigo, which is why I don't always want to be in thought. Thought is like a bad habit, though bad habits give you the full experience of life's flavor, which is the reason I sometimes want to be in thought.

我要求萝卜、白菜与我一同思想，我要求鸡鸭牛羊与我一同思想。思想是一种欲望，我要求所有的禁欲主义者承认这一点，我也要求所有的纵欲主义者认识到这一点。

那些运动员，运动，运动，直到把自己运动垮了为止。那些看到太多事物的人，只好变成瞎子。为了停止思想，你只好拼命思想。思想到变成一个白痴，也算没有白白托生为一个人。

穷尽一个人，这是尼采的工作。穷尽一个人，就是让他变成超人，就是让他拔掉所有的避雷针，并且把自己像避雷针一样挑在大地之上。

关于思想的原则：1，在闹市上思想是一回事，在溪水边思想是另一回事。2，思想不是填空练习，思想是另起炉灶。3，思想到极致的人，即使他悲观厌世，他也会独自鼓掌大笑。

2004，2，20

皮肤颂

枕头的褶皱压在皮肤上。小虫子的小爪子在皮肤上留下印迹。拔火罐从皮肤之下拔出血点。有毒的血点。

I demand that turnips, bok choy, and I all be in thought together, I demand that chickens and ducks and cows and sheep and I all be in thought together. Thought is a kind of desire, and I demand that all ascetics admit it, and I demand that all hedonists recognize it.

Those exercising athletes, they exercise and exercise till they collapse from so much exercise. Those people who see too much, they'd best go blind. To stop being in thought, you'd best think as much as you can. Think until you go stupid, so your incarnation as a person has not been in vain.

The depletion of a person, this was Nietzsche's work. To deplete a person, that is, to make him a superman, that is, to make him pull out all his lightning rods, and moreover to make him stick like a lightning rod out of the earth.

Regarding the principles of thought: (1) To be in thought in the hustle and bustle of the marketplace is one thing, to be in thought beside a stream is something else. (2) Thought isn't an exercise in filling in blanks, thought is making a fresh start. (3) Someone who has thought ad infinitum, even if he is a pessimistic cynic, will still clap his hands and laugh, and louder laugh all on his own.

20 February 2004

ODE TO SKIN

The creases of the pillow press into the skin. The claws of the insect leave their mark on the skin. Acupressure cupping glasses cup up blood spots from beneath the skin. Poisonous blood spots.

皮肤。我寂静的表层。我这不曾遭受过酷刑的皮肤,幻想着酷刑,就进入了历史,就长出了寂静的庄稼:我这了无历史感的汗毛。

山水画在皮肤上。地图刺在皮肤上。纳粹的人皮灯罩。乔叟时代英格兰的图书封皮用少女乳房的皮肤制成。

沙发,以牛皮为自己的皮肤,却不具有那死去动物的灵魂。每一次从牛皮沙发上站起,我总是忍不住牛鸣三声。

她的皮肤遇到了花朵:杨玉环。她的皮肤遇到了冰:王昭君。那些我永远无法遇到的皮肤,我只是说说而已。

但当我注目我潜伏着血管的皮肤,我也就看见了你清凉在夏季的皮肤。但我还想看见你的骨头。

无耻的骨头,裹着雅洁的皮肤,遇到什么样的皮肤它就会瞬间变得像骨头一样无耻?只有面颊懂得害羞和尴尬。

放大镜下皮肤的纹理。穿衣镜中皮肤的灰暗。麻子、痦子、疣子、鸡皮疙瘩。皮肤只将命运表达给能够读懂命运的人。

我的皮肤内装着我的疾病、快乐和幽暗。我的幽暗是灯光不能照亮的。

Skin. My silent surface. This skin of mine that has never been subjected to cruel punishment, fantasizing about cruel punishment, has entered history, has grown forth silent crops: this fine body hair of mine with no sense of history.

A landscape painting on the skin. A map tattooed on the skin. A Nazi human skin lampshade. A dust jacket from Chaucerian England crafted from the skin of a young girl's breasts.

A sofa, with cow's skin for its own skin, does not contain the soul of that dead animal. Every time I arise from a leather sofa, I can't help but moo three times.

Her skin met with a flower: Courtesan Yang Guifei. Her skin met with ice: Consort Wang Zhaojun. All that skin that I will never meet with, that I'm only just talking about.

But when I focus on the skin concealing my veins, I can see as well your skin cooling in the summertime. But I would also like to see your bones.

Shameless bones, bound in pristine skin, what kind of skin will it meet with to instantly make it as shameless as bone? Only cheeks understand what it is to be shy and awkward.

The grain of skin beneath a microscope. The pallor of the skin in the dressing mirror. Pocks, moles, warts, goose bumps. Skin expresses fate only to those who know how to read fate.

My skin bears my disease, my happiness, and my gloom. My gloom cannot be brightened by lamplight.

永久的七窍。临时性伤口。疼的皮肤。藏起来的皮肤。长在里面的皮肤。失去神经末梢的皮肤。死人的皮肤。

据说鬼魂没有皮肤也东游西逛。

据说太空人用皮肤来思想。

你用皮肤向我靠近，或者我用皮肤感受你的颤抖。我说不准你是否想要揭下我的皮肤去披到狼或者羊的身上。

2006，6

The seven constant apertures. A temporary wound. Skin
that aches. Skin that hides. Skin always inside. Skin that
has lost its nerve endings. Skin of the dead.

It's said that ghosts do not have skin and wander east and west.

It's said that in space they think with their skin.

You get close to me with your skin, or I feel your trembling
with my skin. I can't tell whether you want to peel off my
skin to give to a wolf or a sheep to wear.

June 2006

蝙蝠

蝙蝠在这里，那里
头顶上无数个黑影叠加
顷刻间，我的孤独有了边界

假如我浮上去
和它们一起沐浴
会成为晚霞难以承受的惊人重压

当蝙蝠慢慢拖动霞光
我孤独着，蝙蝠便是我的黑天鹅
无数尖齿鸣叫着催促我的血流

一圈又一圈
它们幸福的希望在哪里？
还是每只蝙蝠都想试用月亮这块滑板？

我开始感到它们振翅的温暖
蝙蝠，害怕孤独的蝙蝠，也许你我错在——
不能交谈，却如此接近

2002

Huang Fan

Huang Fan, born in Hubei Province in 1963, represents the Middle Generation group of poets. A graduate of Nanjing's University of Science and Technology, he has served as editor of the poetry journal *Yangtze Poetry* and as a literature teacher in a Nanjing high school. He has organized a series of poetry festivals and published a number of books.

Translated by John Balcom

BATS

Bats here, there
Countless black shadows piled together overhead
In a moment my loneliness is edged round

If I floated up
To bathe with them
I'd become the astonishing, unbearable weight of the evening clouds

As the bats slowly drag the evening sunlight
I am all alone, the bats are my black swans
Countless sharp teeth screeching to hasten the flow of my blood

Circle after circle
Where do their hopes for happiness lie?
Or does each bat want to ride that skateboard, the moon?

I begin to sense the warmth of their beating wings
Bats, bats that fear solitude, perhaps the problem with you and me is—
Being so close but unable to converse

2002

词汇表

云，有关于这个世界的所有说法
城，囤积着这个世界的所有麻烦
爱情，体现出月亮的所有性情
警察，带走了某个月份的阴沉表情
道德，中年时不堪回首的公理，从它
可以推导出妻子、劳役和笑容
诗歌，诗人一生都在修缮的一座公墓
灰尘，只要不停搅动，没准就会有好运
孤独，所有声音听上去都像一只受伤的鸟鸣
自由，劳役之后你无所适从的空虚
门，打开了还有什么可保险的？
满足，当没有什么属于你，就不会为得失受苦了
刀子，人与人对话的最简洁的方式
发现，不过说出古人心中的难言之隐
方言，从诗人脑海里飘过的一些不生育的云

2003

中年

青春是被仇恨啃过的，布满牙印的骨头
是向荒唐退去的，一团热烈的蒸汽
现在，我的面容多么和善
走过的城市，也可以在心里统统夷平了

从遥远的海港，到近处的钟山
日子都是一样陈旧
我拥抱的幸福，也陈旧得像一位烈妇
我一直被她揪着走……

更多青春的种子也变得多余了
　　　　　即便有一条大河在我的身体里

GLOSSARY

Clouds—all the ways of talking about the world
City—a place for storing all the world's troubles
Love—reflects all the moods of the moon
Police—take away a certain month's gloomy looks
Morality—the truth that one cannot bear to recall in middle age, from
 which can be deduced a wife, hard labor, and a smile
Poetry—the cemetery a poet spends his whole life refurbishing
Dust—as long as you don't stop stirring it up, maybe good luck will come
Solitude—every sound is like the cry of an injured bird
Freedom—the emptiness of being at a loss after completing hard labor
Door—what can be safe once it is open?
Contentment—you will not suffer from loss or gain if nothing belongs
 to you
Knife—the form of conversation that goes right to the point
Discovery—nothing more than articulating a topic painful to the ancients
Dialect—a few infertile clouds floating from a poet's brain

2003

MIDDLE AGE

Youth is a bone gnawed by hate and covered with tooth marks
It's a cloud of fervent steam that retreats into absurdity
Right now, my face is so kind and genial
The cities I have passed through can all be leveled in my mind

From the distant port to Zhongshan nearby
The days alike are all passé
The happiness I have embraced is also as old as a martyred woman
Who always holds me fast as she goes...

More seeds of youth would become superfluous
 Though a mighty river flows through my body

它也一声不响。年轻时喜欢说月亮是一把镰刀
　　　　但现在，它是好脾气的宝石
　　　　面对任何人的询问，它只闪闪发光……

　　　　　　　　　　　　　　　　　　　　　　2004

It makes no sound. When young I liked to say the moon was a sickle
    But now, it is an even-tempered gem
    That simply glitters facing anyone who questions...

2004

冬日的变奏

1. 云 彩
那些白色的超凡入圣的物体
我曾亲眼看见它们溶化在蓝天里
它们是佛罗里达夏季的一片海滩
是科罗拉多峡谷中的一块崖石
或只是一个躯体让我盲目地坠入

2. 音 乐
我听见树木与房舍之间的
早晨的大海缓慢下来
太阳倾身在空气里捕捉
那无法捕捉到的东西

3. 天 井
那闪耀着露珠的绿色草坪
被一条白色的小径分隔
黄叶均匀地撒落下来
来自阿姆斯特丹的蒙德里安
从传说的天井里走过

Cai Tianxin

Cai Tianxin, born in Taizhou, Zhejiang, in 1963, entered Shandong University at the age of fifteen. He began writing poetry when he was a PhD student. He has published more than ten collections of poetry, essays, and translations, editions in several foreign languages, as well as a memoir. He teaches at Zhejiang University.

Translated by Kuo-ch'ing Tu
(with assistance from Robert Backus)

VARIATIONS ON A WINTER'S DAY

1. CLOUDS

Those white supernatural hallowed objects
I have personally seen them dissolve into the blue
They are a stretch of summer beach in Florida
a jutting crag in a Colorado canyon
or simply a body that lets me blindly fall in

2. MUSIC

I hear between the trees and the houses
the early morning ocean slowing down
The sun leans into the air to capture
something uncapturable

3. COURTYARD

The green lawn sparkling with drops of dew
is divided by a footpath traced in white
An even sprinkling of yellow leaves
comes from Mondrian in Amsterdam
across the legendary courtyard

4．扇尾鸟

一只过路的长尾鸟栖息在屋顶上
轻捷的脚步，美丽无比的羽毛
又一个夜晚潜伏在我的身后
她凝望着我庄严神圣犹如
碧空凝望着大海，大海凝望着月影

5．女 子

长长的指甲之夜
一双被风吹散的眼睛
我在你的鼻梁上
发现了夏威夷

1993，加利福尼亚

4. FANTAILED BIRD

A passing long-tailed bird is perched on the roof
springy steps   feathers of incomparable beauty
lurking behind me another night
She gazes at me   solemn and sacred the likeness
of an emerald sky gazing at the ocean
and the ocean gazes at the moon's shadow

5. A GIRL

A night of long fingernails
a pair of eyes blown away by the wind
atop the bridge of your nose
I discover Hawaii

1993, California

世界观协会

底线像晾衣绳。
一整天，短裤，裙子，枕套，
胸衣，袜子，滴着湿乎乎的小辫子，
没轻没重地压着它。快要晒干时，
一场不大不小的雷雨
又心血来潮，跑下来察看
我们的邻居新制作出的几个盆景——
从万年青到仙人球，各种植物
向一手绝活报到，企求
在完美的缺陷中获得永生。
又过了一天，看上去更阴沉的
被罩，毯子，毛巾被，床单，
滴着叮当乱响的水珠，压得它
暗无天日。它被拉拽得确实挺狠，
它身上仅有的灵性告诉我们
它是用两根跳绳改成的。
终于在立夏那一天，它细长的肩上
已见不到任何衣物。
它悠闲在那里，轻得就像从火鸡身上
抽出的一根肠子，它哼着空气之歌。

Zang Di

Zang Di was born in Beijing in 1964. He entered Peking University in 1987, completing his education in 1997 with a PhD in literature. Currently an associate professor of Chinese at Peking University, he is a member of the Modern Poetry Institute and editor of *Xinshi pinglun*. His work has won several major prizes, including the 2000 Writer Magazine Poetry Prize.

Translated by Christopher Lupke

A CONVENTION ON WORLDVIEWS

A baseline is like a clothesline.
All day long, shorts, skirts, pillowcases,
Brassieres, stockings, a dripping-wet little braid,
Relentlessly pulling it down. When just about dried in the sun,
A medium-sized thunderstorm
Impulsively rises up; running down to examine
The potted landscape that our neighbors created—
From evergreens to cacti, all sorts of plants
Reporting for duty with their unique skills, hoping to derive eternal life
From their perfect flaws.
Another day passed, and it looked as though the weightier
Quilt covers, blankets, terry coverlets, and sheets,
With the noisy cascade of dripping water, pressed it
Into total darkness. It really was being pulled ruthlessly,
The mere spirit of its body told us
It had been converted from two jump ropes.
Finally, on the first day of summer, on its long, thin shoulders
One could no longer see any laundry.
It just loitered there, as light as guts
Yanked from a turkey, it hummed a song.

不过很快，三只麻雀就结伴而来，
旁若无人地，踩着它的歌喉。

火山学丛书

我们相互缠绕就如同这木兰树
用它的根去呼吸。这地下活动的范围很广，
对象也很驳杂，牵连到爱的秘密，
复活的秘密，春天的启示，
以及心灵的可怕的无辜。你是否愿意

我们的秘密仅仅是一个契约。
神圣的契约，没有引号，它送给你的火山
一个突出的形状。端详它时，
它是魔术师正用着的灯罩。一旦凑近到
不能再近，它就是小王子刚闻过的玉兰花。

引擎强大得像岩浆离地面
还有十米：它随时都会爆发，
为了治疗得更彻底。所以，每个乐园的深处
都该有一座火山。蘑菇云下面
没有蘑菇，但你不必担心缺少装饰和午餐。

荒地已被开垦出来，除了小青菜，
还种植了高大的落叶乔木。先有花，后有叶，
甚至不必做梦，也会有花露嘀嗒。
树皮剥下来就是药。你吃过，你才会想起
你已经很久没下过一个决心了。

But very quickly, three sparrows converged on it,
Self-assured, tramping on its voice.

A COMPENDIUM OF VOLCANOLOGY

Our intertwining is like this magnolia tree
Breathing through its roots. The underground activity has a wide range,
And the objects of its intention are quite diverse, involving the secrets
     of love
And of resurrection, the revelation of spring,
As well as the frightful innocence of the spirit. Would you prefer it if

Our secrets were no more than a contract?
A hallowed contract, no quotation marks, a volcano given to you,
A protruding object. If you study it closely,
It is a magician's lampshade. Once you get closer,
As close as you can, it becomes magnolia blossoms a prince has just
     smelled.

An engine so powerful it's like magma ten meters
From the earth's surface: it could explode at any time,
In order to cure more thoroughly. So, in the depth of all pleasure gardens
There should be a volcano. Beneath the mushroom cloud
There are no mushrooms, but you needn't worry about a lack of
     adornment or lunch.

The wasteland has been cultivated, besides some small vegetables
Tall, deciduous trees have been planted. First there were blossoms,
     then leaves,
There's no need even to dream, the dew will drip and drop.
Bark peeled from the trees is medicine. If you ate it, you'd realize
It's been a long, long time since you set your mind to anything.

亚洲铜

亚洲铜，亚洲铜
祖父死在这里，父亲死在这里，我也会死在这里
你是唯一的一块埋人的地方

亚洲铜，亚洲铜
爱怀疑和爱飞翔的是鸟，淹没一切的是海水
你的主人却是青草，住在自己细小的腰上，守住野花的手掌和秘密

亚洲铜，亚洲铜
看见了吗？那两只白鸽子，它们是屈原遗落在沙滩上的白鞋子
让我们——我们和河流一起，穿上它们吧

亚洲铜，亚洲铜
击鼓之后，我们把在黑暗中跳舞的心脏叫作月亮
这月亮主要由你构成

1984

Hai Zi

Hai Zi, birth name Zha Haisheng, was born in 1964 in the village of Zha Bay in Anhui Province. In 1979, he entered the law department of Peking University. In March 1989, he killed himself by lying on railroad tracks at Shanhaiguan. In the twenty-two years since his death, he has become a poet of unmatched renown.

Translated by Gerald Maa

ASIAN BRONZE

Asian bronze, Asian bronze
Grandfathers die here, fathers die here, I will also die here
You are the only plot of land for buried men

Asian bronze, Asian bronze
What loves to doubt and fly is the bird, what floods everything is the sea
Yet your master is green grass, living on its own slender waist, looking
    after the secrets and palms of wildflowers

Asian bronze, Asian bronze
Have you seen it? Those two doves, they are the white shoes Qu Yuan
    lost on the sandy beach
Let us—us together with the river—put them on

Asian bronze, Asian bronze
After the drumming, we called the heart dancing in the darkness
    the moon
This moon is mainly shaped by you

1984

最后一夜和第一日的献诗

今夜你的黑头发
是岩石上寂寞的黑夜
牧羊人用雪白的羊群
填满飞机场周围的黑暗

黑夜比我更早睡去
黑夜是神的伤口
你是我的伤口
羊群和花朵也是岩石的伤口

雪山 用大雪填满飞机场周围的黑暗
雪山女神吃的是野兽穿的是鲜花
今夜 九十九座雪山高出天堂
使我彻夜难眠

1989，1, 16–24

黑夜的献诗

献给黑夜的女儿

黑夜从大地上升起
遮住了光明的天空
丰收后荒凉的大地
黑夜从你内部上升

你从远方来，我到远方去
遥远的路程经过这里
天空一无所有
为何给我安慰

A POEM DEDICATED TO THE FINAL NIGHT
AND THE FIRST DAY

Tonight your black hair
Is a lonesome night upon a rock
Shepherds use snow-white herds
To fill the darkness circling the airport

The night falls asleep earlier than I
The night is a god's wound
You are my wound
Sheep and flowers are also the rock's wounds

Snow mountains   use heavysnow to fill the darkness circling the
      airport
What the snow mountain goddess eats are beasts, wears are fresh
      flowers
Tonight   ninety-nine snow mountains tower above heaven
Make me restless all night

16–24 January 1989

A POEM DEDICATED TO THE DARK NIGHT
for the night's daughter

The dark night rises from the earth
Blocks out the bright sky
The earth desolate after a rich harvest
The dark night arises from your interior

You come from a distant place, I go to a distant place
The long journey passes here
The sky has nothing
Why does it give me comfort

丰收之后荒凉的大地
人们取走了一年的收成
取走了粮食骑走了马
留在地里的人，埋得很深

草叉闪闪发亮，稻草堆在火上
稻谷堆在黑暗的谷仓
谷仓中太黑暗，太寂静，太丰收
也太荒凉，我在丰收中看到了阎王的眼睛

黑雨滴一样的鸟群
从黄昏飞入黑夜
黑夜一无所有
为何给我安慰

走在路上
放声歌唱
大风刮过山冈
上面是无边的天空

1989，2，2

The earth desolate after a rich harvest
People took away a year's worth of crops
Took away grain, rode horses away
People left in the ground, buried very deep

A pitchfork shines, rice-straw heaps on the fire
Rice heaps in the granary
The granary too dark, too still, too plentiful
And too bleak, I caught sight of Yama's eyes in the bumper crop

A bird flock like dark raindrops
Flying from dusk into the night
The dark night has nothing
Why does it give me comfort

Walking on a road
Singing out loud
A gale blows past the low hills
Above is a boundless sky

2 February 1989

一棵葡萄

在街上，一个美丽的妇人
向我抱怨她单调的梦，而我告诉她
应该在她常梦到的地方
植一株葡萄

我说：它将长势旺盛
抽出新芽
并且会很快攀上旁边一棵年老的榆树
要么，缠住一块石头
因此一切会有所不同

要知道，人在这世上
会有另一样东西和他承受
相同的命运

你信不信。你的乳房也将再次充盈
当它长出星小的果实时
但一只黑鸟会突如其来地啄食

简直如同闪电
一只黑鸟，来自百里之外一个男人的梦境
并且已被豢养了多年

Ye Hui

Ye Hui, a native of Gaochun County, Jiangsu Province, was born in 1964. He is the author of one collection of poetry.

Translated by Michael Gibbs Hill

A GRAPEVINE

Out on the street, a beautiful woman
complained to me about her humdrum dreams
                                        so I told her:
You should plant a grapevine
in a place you often dream of

I said: It will thrive and flourish
                            and sprout new buds
and quickly climb the aged elm beside it
or knot itself around a stone
Because of this, everything will be changed

You must understand, people in this world
will find things with a different form
that share the same fate

do you believe it. Your breast will grow full again
And when it bears tiny fruit
a black bird will come from nowhere to peck and eat it

just like lightning
A black bird, one from the dreams of a man
                                    a hundred miles away
one kept and caged for years

我不能告诉你他是谁，住在何处
因为一旦说出来，某个院子里
疯长的荒草就会死去

遗传

我上班的地方
有一张五十年代的
办公桌。平时
我把脚架上去
当有人来时，我就移开
让他们看
桌沿上的压痕：一道很深的
腿的压痕
人们往往会惊讶道
如此逼真
而我告诉他们
这不是我一个人的缘故
还有其他人
它以前的主人，是
集体创造
就像楼上那个女同事
她有一双漂亮的眼睛
那也同样不是她的
独创，那可能是她母亲的
也可能是她祖母的
甚至有可能
是我爷爷的一个伯父的，它们
一代接着
一代

I cannot tell you who he is
                    where he lives
Because if I speak those words, the weeds growing wild
in a courtyard somewhere
                    will die out

INHERITANCE

Where I work
there's a desk
from the fifties. Usually
I put my feet up on it
but when someone comes by
I'll move my feet aside
to let him see
the indentation on the edge of the desk: a deep
rut in the shape of a leg
people are always shocked and say
it's so vivid
but I tell them
it's not just from me
there were others
its previous owners, it's
a collective creation
just like the woman who works upstairs
she has a pair of beautiful eyes
those, too, are not her own
creation, they could be from her mother
or maybe her grandmother
or perhaps even from
one of my father's uncles
                    they
are passed down generation
to generation

奇妙的收藏

每天我都希望能为我的收藏
增加些什么：硬币，揉皱的纸币，一瓶子空气
一些词语和一些破碎的句子
事物和事物的名称杂乱地堆放在一起
有时它们会互相混淆
一些纸币失踪了，你能在纸上找到
"一些纸币被抚平后买了冰冻天使"
那是一种冰淇淋的名字
常常是这样：肥皂，"喉管"
组成了——"一块肥皂卡在夏天的喉管里"
而"理智"和"工棚"则自动组成
"理智可怕的工棚"，出现在一页书中
有一天我发现自己像一个小贩
默默穿过低矮的工棚

事物不断地变成词语，消失
实体的钥匙插入词语的锁孔
打开的是语言的抽屉
未完成的诗，写好待发的信，照片背后的题辞
它们介于词和实体之间

Ma Yongbo

Ma Yongbo was born in Yichun, Heilongjiang, in 1964. Since 1986, Ma has published over forty original works and translations. He is an associate professor in the Faculty of Humanities and Social Sciences, Nanjing University of Science and Technology, and a leading scholar in Anglo-American postmodernist poetry.

Translated by Chi Yu Chu

A MYSTERIOUS COLLECTION

Every day I hope I can add to my collection
Some items: coins, crumpled paper money, a bottle of air
Some words and broken sentences
Piled-up objects and names of things
Sometimes all mixed up
Some paper money disappears, and you can find on a note
"Some smoothed-out paper money spent on Frozen Angel"
The name of an ice cream
It is often like this: soap, "throat"
Forming—"a piece of soap stuck in summer's *throat*"
But "reason" and "work shed" automatically form
"A dreadful work shed of reason," appearing on the page of a book
One day I find myself like a hawker
Silently passing through a low work shed

Things keep turning into words, and disappearing
The key of substance put into the keyhole of words
To open the drawer of language
An unfinished poem, a letter to be mailed, inscription on the back of
    a photo
Are between words and substance

需要一双阅读的眼睛以变成完全的词语
"抽屉里没有蛇"，那就是说
抽屉里没有蛇，却有蛇的副本
无害，却足以让我发冷
让我听见它吸气的声音
这和房间里没有女人有些类似
但生活并不因此变得简单
如果你的女友突然失踪
你会在我的抽屉里找到她
不过她已被拆成了不相关的部分：
大腿，脸蛋，胸，毛发
已经没有可供辨别的个性
诸如眼波的流转，和腰肢的轻盈

大地上的事物越来越少
而我的野心不是很大
下一次我收藏的是一座料场
和一个正在拆除的煤气公司
那些玩具似的红色汽车有秩序地进进退退
我已观察了很久：它们一直
在把生锈的铁搬到最靠里的地方
那些工人还没有发觉
他们已变成了动词
一直把名词们搬来搬去
他们已不能拿到可以流通的货币

装满细沙的瓶子在窗台上旋转
我每天都梦见沙子又多了一粒
要慢慢把我埋住
从那样的梦中惊醒，我决定
让一些词语再转化成事物：
让诗变成铅字和纸币
把瓶子和沙子分头抛进江心
当一切停止，我发现
我也是寂静收藏的一个词语

They need a pair of reading eyes to turn into complete language
"There's no snake in the drawer," that means
There's no snake in the drawer, but a copy of it
Harmless, but sending chills down my spine
Making me hear the sound of its breath
It is like no woman in the room
But it doesn't make life simpler
If your girlfriend suddenly disappears
You will find her in my drawer
Only disintegrated into irrelevant parts
Leg, face, chest, hair
Without identifiable character
Such as the turning of the eyes, or graceful movements of the hips

Things on earth are fewer and fewer
I am not someone with great ambition
The next item in my collection will be a store yard
And a gas company that's being torn down
The toylike red trucks going back and forth in an orderly fashion
I've been watching for a while: they keep
Moving rusty metal into the farthest corners
The workmen have not realized
That they have turned into verbs
Moving nouns around
They can no longer earn real money

The bottle filled with fine sand spins on the windowsill
Every day I dream one more grain of sand added
Aiming to slowly bury me
Waking up from a dream like that, I decide
To let words and expressions turn back into things
Let poetry turn into typefaces and paper money
Throw the bottle and sand separately into the heart of the river
When everything stands still, I find
I, too, am a word collected by silence

马甸桥

24小时。连续24小时——
这是昼和夜加在一起的分量。

在桥边，一个人滋生危险的念头。
一天一天，你伤害了多少时光！

在每一个路口，危险和危险擦肩而过。

桥上所见的纷乱，
桥下所承受的震动……

生活，在路上。家庭只是
停靠站。轮胎冒烟，出汗，滚烫……

迟早的车祸粉碎了对前途的算计。

从这边看，又从那边看，
马甸桥没有内部，只是空穴。

Shu Cai

Shu Cai (Chen Shucai) was born in Zhejiang in 1965. He graduated from Beijing Foreign Studies University in 1987, majoring in French. From 1990 to 1994, he was a diplomat at the Chinese Embassy in Senegal. In 2000, he joined the Foreign Literature Research Institute at the Chinese Academy of Social Sciences. He has published both poetry and essays, and his writing has been translated into many languages. He has translated various French poets into Chinese, including Reverdy, Char, and Bonnefoy. He lives in Beijing.

Translated by Diana Shi
and George O'Connell

MADIAN BRIDGE

24 hours. Hour after hour,
each day's weight, each night's.

At the bridge rail, someone breeds dark thoughts.
Day after day, so much wounded time!

At each crossroads, danger rubs shoulders with danger.

On the bridge, traffic's turmoil.
Below, tremor and rumbling load.

Life, a highway. Family
a brief stop. Tires smoldering, sweating, scalding hot.

Sooner or later, an accident smashes the plan.

From this side or that
Madian Bridge has no interior, only an empty arch.

过路的红裙，上下颤动的乳房，
松柏的生长缺乏氧气……

茶树用浑圆理解形式主义。

24小时。连续24小时——
小轿车，自行车，马车，重型卡车……

危险的预感逼迫人一次次出门。
推迟那个梦，或在梦中醒着！

有什么更好的办法对付这噪音？

还得把生活挣来，
还得把肉和蔬菜拎上楼……

1996

安宁

我想写出此刻的安宁
我心中枯草一样驯服的安宁
被风吹送着一直升向天庭的安宁
我想写出这住宅小区的安宁
汽车开走了停车场空荡荡的安宁
儿童们奔跑奶奶们闲聊的安宁
我想写出这风中的清亮的安宁
草茎颤动着咝咝响的安宁
老人裤管里瘦骨的安宁
我想写出这泥地上湿乎乎的安宁
阳光铺出的淡黄色的安宁
断枝裂隙间干巴巴的安宁
我想写出这树影笼罩着的安宁
以及树影之外的安宁

The red skirt passing by, the trembling breasts,
for pine and cypress, not enough air.

Tea trees embrace their formal spheres.

24 hours. Hour after hour,
cars, bicycles, horse carts, heavy trucks.

Again and again fear drives us from the house.
Put off your dream, or wake in it.

How else to deal with this racket?

Still have to make a living.
Still have to lug upstairs the vegetables, the meat.

1996

TRANQUILITY

I want to set down the tranquility of this moment,
tranquility tame as the grass withered in my heart,
tranquility lofted by wind toward heaven.
I want to set down the tranquility of this compound,
the tranquility of its parking lot emptied of cars,
the tranquility of children running, grandmothers chatting.
I want to set down the clear and bright tranquility of the breeze,
the whispered tranquility of the weedstalk, shivering,
the bony tranquility of old people's pantlegs.
I want to set down the damp tranquility of muddy ground,
the flaxen tranquility of spread sunlight,
the dry tranquility within the splintered branch.
I want to set down the tranquility shrouded by tree shade,
and the tranquility beyond the shade,

以及天地间青蓝色的安宁
我这么想着没功夫再想别的
我这么想着一路都这么想着
占据我全身心的，就是这
——安宁

2000

from earth to sky this green-to-blue tranquility.
Thinking this, I think of nothing else.
Thinking this, it overwhelms me,
soul and body, this
—tranquility.

2000

毛

这些日子
我在读一本海外出版的
毛泽东传
每天读上那么几章

有好几次
读着读着
我竟哑然失笑
那是想起了
一位过去的老哥
我吃惊地发现
他在很多地方
都在刻意学毛
思维方式
说话口气
表演习惯
我发现这样的老哥
其实还有很多
充斥在我的四周
甚至于我的父亲
也是其中的一个

Yi Sha

Yi Sha, whose real name is Wu Wenjian, was born in 1966 in Chengdu, Sichuan Province. A 1989 graduate of Beijing Normal University with a major in Chinese, he holds an academic position at Xi'an Foreign Languages University.

Translated by Mabel Lee

MAO

Lately
I've been reading a foreign publication
A biography of Mao Zedong
Getting through a few chapters each day

Quite a few times
While reading away
I couldn't help chuckling
Because it reminded me
That there was this guy
I was surprised to discover
Who in many respects
Was painstakingly copying Mao's
Way of thinking
Tone of voice
Habit of acting
I discovered that this sort of guy
In fact existed in large numbers
There were lots of them all around me
And even my father
Was among them

读到后来
我发现了自己
与他们有所不同
而更为可怕的是
我其实并未刻意去学
但竟然还是很像

2008

无题（77）

正月十五
是舅舅该给
外甥送灯笼的日子
从中国的民俗
我想到我那
美国的外甥
英文名叫艾瑞克
中文名叫万小宇
纯种华裔
同时见过我俩者
无不说他长得
跟我儿时
一个球样
调皮捣蛋的个性也像
连公鸭嗓子都像
表现欲很强
人来疯
这又应了一句
中国的俗语
"外甥随舅"
生在美国喝纽约州的
免费牛奶长大的小宇
电话里永远呜哩哇啦
只会说英语的艾瑞克

As I read on
I discovered that I
Was different from them
And even more frightening that
Without any painstaking copying
I was really just like him

2008

UNTITLED (77)

On the 15th of the first month
Maternal uncles give gifts of lanterns to
Their maternal nephews
This Chinese folk custom
Makes me think of my
American maternal nephew
Called Eric in English
And Wan Xiaoyu in Chinese
With 100 percent Chinese ancestry
Anyone who has seen the two of us together
Always says he looks
Bloody hell like I did
As a child
His mischievous character is the same
Even his raspy voice is the same
He is a big show-off
And goes crazy if there are visitors
So proving
The Chinese saying that
"Maternal nephews are like their maternal uncles"
Xiaoyu, who was born in America and
Grew up drinking New York State's free milk
Always speaks gibberish on the phone

舅舅现在想的是如何
将中国的灯笼送给你
我在电脑上画了一个
热气球般飞行的灯笼
现在就给你发过去
请你用自由女神手中的火炬
把它点亮

2009

Eric, who can only speak English
Your maternal uncle has been thinking of how
To give you a Chinese lantern So on the computer I've sketched
A lantern like a hot-air balloon
That I am sending to you now
I want you to use the Statue of Liberty's torch
To light it up

2009

刺猬论

冬天冷，我们花一天时间
讨论刺猬。
我们在房子里，开着空调，
穿着运动衫，心里柔软。

刺猬怀孕了，
刺猬误入农民的院子，
刺猬逻辑混乱，生下一窝小刺猬。
小刺猬爬。我们讨论得很认真。

假设一只光秃秃的小刺猬一个肉团滚到
我们的脚下或者直接爬到我们的床上在
你我之间讨论的间隙或者梦中，我们还
继续讨论吗？

当然。
我们会沮丧，
夜不能寐而伸手于窗外。
我们可以讨论更现实的问题：我们。

Yu Nu

Yu Nu was born in 1966 in Anqing, Anhui Province. He graduated from Shanghai University of Electric Power. He has published more than six collections and won the Gold Prize in the first Gemini Poetry Competition in Taiwan, another award in the second Poetry Competition, and the Mingtian-Erguna Award from the poetry magazine *Tomorrow*.

Translated by Terry Siu-han Yip

ON HEDGEHOGS

In the winter cold, we spent a day
Talking about hedgehogs
In the house, with the air conditioner on,
In sport shirts, with tender hearts.

The hedgehog was pregnant,
Went astray and got into a farmer's yard,
Confused, gave birth to a kennel of little hedgehogs.
The crawling little ones. Our earnest discussions.

Suppose a hairless little hedgehog rolling like a meatball
Ended up at our feet or crawled straight onto our bed during
Short breaks in our discussions, or in our dreams, would we
Continue with our discussion?

Certainly.
We would feel depressed,
On our sleepless nights, we stretch our hands out the window.
We could discuss a more practical issue: us.

目睹

早晨的空气被抽掉了，大麻造成的不愉快
使他和她互相取代。远处，一个玩球的少年
不见了，河面上漂着他的帽子，软组织像
割断的水藻一样，无人过问。那是７６年
我一个人住在花园里，才１０岁，夜里
我害怕极了（你听见过夜间花开的
声音吗？），同时我看见
一条鱼，在福尔马林里游来游去
那一刻我有着瓶子一样的预感：他和她
眼睛和躯干，两个盲人的机械装置
将在花园里被拆散，植物的苦闷
都是这样，心里明白，却说不出口
直到一朵花出现，或卖血为生的妇人
在血中隐匿，躲在那里，永不露面
像我二十年后所做的，用雨水说话
描写那一年的十一月，用调匀的颜色
说，用伸缩着的阴影说。在惊呆的月光下
他站着，二十年了，她呼吸的灰尘
还围绕着他，她的脸
被一把锁锁着，看不清，也没有留下
一张照片，从那时起，我就只相信感官
她是鸟走后留下的尸体，是一张纸上
残存的理性之肉
随风飘着，纯属捏造。现在我回来了
那个少年却没有回来，花园里
找不到他的骨骸。两个人
埋伏在一个人的身上，多少年不发一语
他们想干什么？由此我肯定
我是一只混蛋月亮，把什么都看在眼里
在草丛中，在堆放着旧轮胎的小径上

WITNESS

With the morning air drawn away, the unpleasantness of marijuana
Made him and her replace each other. At a distance, a youth playing ball
Disappeared, his cap floating on the river, the soft tissues
Like cut seaweed, abandoned. That was 1976.
I lived alone in the garden, just turned ten. At night
I was scared. (Have you heard flowers bloom at night,
The sound of it?) I also saw
A fish, flowing to and fro in formalin.
At that moment I had a premonition as clear as the bottle: he and she
Eyes and bodies, two blind persons' mechanical devices
Would be disassembled in the garden. The dejection of plants
Was such, crystal clear at heart, but unable to say a word
Until a flower appeared, or a woman selling blood for a living
Hid in blood; hiding there, never showing her face
Like what I did twenty years later. Speaking through the rain
Of that bygone November; depicting it with well-mixed colors,
Describing it with changing shades. Under the terrified moonlight,
He had stood, for twenty years, the dust she breathed in still circling
        him; her face
Fastened on a lock, obscure, without leaving behind
A picture. From then on, I believed only in the senses—
She was the carcass left behind by a bird, the remains of the intellect
On a piece of paper—
Fluttering in the wind, sheer fabrication. Now I am back
But not that young man. In the garden
No trace of his bones. Two persons
Hidden in one body, kept silent for years.
What did they want to do? I could be sure from this
That I am a good-for-nothing moon, witnessing everything
In the grass, on a side path stacked with used tires.

献给黄昏的星

黄昏的星从大地的海洋升起
我站在黑夜的尽头
看到黄昏像一座雪白的裸体
我是天空中唯一一颗发光的星星

在这艰难的时刻
我仿佛看到了另一种人类的昨天
三个相互残杀的事物被怼到了一起
黄昏，是天空中唯一的发光体
星，是黑夜的女儿苦闷的床单
我，是我一生中无边的黑暗

在这最后的时刻，我竟能梦见
这荒芜的大地，最后一粒种子
这下垂的时间，最后一个声音
这个世界，最后的一件事情，黄昏的星

1990，4，11

Ge Mai

Ge Mai is the pen name of Chu Fujun. Born in Heilongjiang in 1967, he studied Chinese literature and graduated from Peking University in 1989 with a BA. He then worked for the journal *Chinese Literature*. On 24 September 1991, he drowned himself. His poetry was first published in 1993, followed by his collected poems in 1999. Ge Mai summed up his poetics with these words: "Poetry belongs to the domain of the imagination; it... makes possible the impossible."

Translated by Michelle Yeh

A STAR DEDICATED TO NIGHTFALL

The evening star rises from the ocean of the earth
I stand on the edge of the dark night to see
The twilight like a snow-white naked body
I am the only shining star in the sky

At this difficult moment
I have the vision of the yesterday of another humankind
The three that try to kill one another are thrown together:
Nightfall, the only glowing object in the sky
Star, the distressed bedding of night's daughter
And I, the endless darkness of my life

At this final moment, I can still dream
Of the last seed in the barren earth
The last voice of descending time
The last thing in the world, the evening star

11 April 1990

死后看不见阳光的人

死后看不见阳光的人，是不幸的人
他们是一队白袍的天使被摘光了脑袋
抑郁地在修道院的小径上来回走动
并小声合唱，这种声音能够抵达
塔檐下乌鸦们针眼大小袖珍的耳朵

那些在道路上梦见粪便的黑羊
能够看见发丛般浓密的白杨，而我作为
一条丑恶的鞭子
抽打着这些诋咒死亡的意象
那便是一面旗，它作为黑暗而飞舞

死后，谁还能再看见阳光，生命
作为庄严的替代物，它已等候很久
明眸填满了褐色羊毛
可以成为一片夜晚的星光
我们在死后看不到熔岩内溅出的火光

死后我们不能够梦见梦见诗歌的人
这仿佛是一个魔瓶乖巧的入口
飞旋的昆虫和对半裂开的种子
都能够使我们梦见诗歌，而诗歌中
晦暗的文字，就是死后看不见阳光的人们

1991，7，12

THOSE WHO CAN'T SEE SUNLIGHT
AFTER THEY DIE

Those who can't see sunlight after they die are unfortunate souls
They are a troop of headless angels in white robes
Depressed, they walk back and forth on a narrow path at the monastery
Singing in chorus in a voice so low that it can only reach
The crows under the pagoda eaves, their ears as small as the eye of
      a needle

Those black sheep on the road dream of shit
They can see aspens as dense as hair, and I
Am an evil whip
Flogging images that curse at death
A dancing banner of darkness

Who can still see sunlight after death? Life
As a solemn substitute has waited so long
Bright eyes are filled with brown wool
They can turn into starlight in the night
Lava sparks that we can't see after we die

After we die we can't dream of those who dream of poetry
Like the clever mouth of the magic bottle
All the flying bugs and seeds that crack in the middle
Will enable us to dream of poetry, whose obscure words
Are those who can't see sunlight after they die

12 July 1991

浮云

仰望晴空，五月的晴空，麦垛的晴空
天空中光的十字，白虎在天空漫游
宗教在天空漫游，虎的额头向大地闪亮
额头上的王字向大地闪亮

恒河之水在天上漂，沙粒臻露锋芒
黑色的披风，黑色的星，圆木沉实而雄壮
一只白象迎面而来，像南亚的荷花
荷叶围困池水，池水行在天上

遗忘之声落落寡欢，背着两只大脑
一只是爱琴海的阳光，一只是犹太的王
良知的手紧紧托住一只废黜的大脑
失恋的脑，王位与圣杯在森林中游荡

云朵是一群群走过呵，向西，向海洋
在主公的坟头，在死者的鼻梁
一名法官安坐其上，他的胡须安坐其上
一只牧羊犬悔恨地投诉着泪水的故乡

泪水的故乡，泪水之乡也是心愿之乡
心愿在河上摆渡，不能说生活是妄想
遗忘的摇篮，遗忘的谷仓
一个秃头的儿子伫立河上，秃头闪闪发亮

1991，8

FLOATING CLOUD

Look up at the sunny sky, the sunny sky of May, the sunny sky of
     wheat stacks
A cross of light in the sky, where a white tiger roams
Religion roams, the tiger's forehead twinkles at the earth
The word *king* on its forehead twinkles at the earth

The waters of the Ganges float in the sky, grains of sand gleam sharply
Black capes, black stars, logs heavy and majestic
A white elephant approaches, like a lotus flower from South Asia
The pond is stranded by the lotus leaves, its water walks in the sky

The lonely sound of oblivion carries two brains on its back:
One is the sunlight of the Aegean Sea, the other the King of the Jews
The hands of conscience tightly cup a banished brain
The brain of jilted love, the throne, and the chalice roam the forest

Clouds pass by in a crowd, to the west, to the ocean
By the tomb of the master, on the nose ridge of the deceased
A judge sits squarely, his mustache sits squarely
A shepherd dog complains ruefully about the homeland of tears

The homeland of tears is also the homeland of wishes
They ferry across the river, one can't say life is a delusion
The cradle of oblivion, the granary of oblivion
A son stands still on the river, his bald head shining

August 1991

未完成的途中

……午夜。一行字呼啸着
冲出黑暗的隧道。幽蓝的信号灯
闪过。一列拖着脐带的火车
穿越桥梁，枕木下
我凹陷的前胸不断震颤。它紧抵
俯身降落的天空，碾平，伸展
——你知道，我

总是这样，摇晃着
在深夜起身，喝口水
坐下。信。电话线中嗡嗡的雪原。躺在
键盘上被自己的双手运走。翻山越岭
从水杉的尖顶上沉沉扫过，枝条
划破饥渴的脸。或者，贴着地面

Lan Lan

Lan Lan was born in 1967 in Shandong Province. She has worked as a factory laborer and a literary editor. In addition to poetry, she has published six collections of prose and six collections of children's stories, including full-length fairy tales. In 1996 she received the Liu Li-an Poetry Prize. In 2005 she was named one of the top ten young women poets in China. In 2008 the magazine *Poetry and People* gave her its poetry prize.

Translated by Mike O'Connor

UNFINISHED JOURNEY

...Midnight. A line of words
whistling streaks from a dark tunnel.
(A signal lamp had flashed—dark blue.)
The train, pulling cars by an umbilical cord,
crosses the trestle, and below the tracks,
my chest sinks—I can't stop trembling.
Resisting the bending, falling sky, the train
flattens, stretches out.
—You know, I

am always this way, shaking,
getting up in the night, drinking water,
sitting down. Mail. The snowy field
in the hum of the phone line. My hands
on the keyboard send mail traveling
over mountains and valleys. Rough-
swept branches from the tops
of dawn redwoods scratch my needy face,
or maybe, close to the ground,
there are ice crystals sticking,

冰碴挂上眉毛，你知道，有时

我走在纬四路的楝树下，提着青菜
推门，仿佛看到你的背影，孩子们快乐尖叫
冲过来抱着我的腿。雨从玻璃上滴落。
屋子晃动起来，轮子无声地滑行
拖着傍晚的炊烟。那时，市声压低了

楼下的钉鞋匠，取出含在嘴里的钉子
抡起铁锤，狠狠地楔进生活的鞋底，毫不
犹豫。这些拾荒的人
拉着破烂的架子车，藏起捡到的分币
粗大的骨节从未被摧毁。

你知道，端午时节
蒿草浓烈的香气中，我们停靠的地方
布谷鸟从深夜一直叫到天亮，在远处的林子里
躲在树荫下面。你睫毛长长的眼睛
闭着。手边是放凉的水杯和灰烬的余烟。
站在窗前，
我想：我爱这个世界。在那
裂开的缝隙里，我有过机会。
它缓缓驶来，拐了弯……

hanging on my eyebrows.
You know, sometimes

I walk beneath japonicas on Wei Si Road
carrying green vegetables, push
open the door and seem to see you
from behind. The children happily shouting
rush to me, embrace my legs. Rain
drips on the windowpane. The room
starts shaking with the quiet
gliding passage of wheels
towing the evening kitchen smoke.
Then the noise of the city falls.

Downstairs a cobbler takes a nail
from his mouth and, wielding a hammer
without hesitation, drives it
fiercely into the sole of life.
These *shihuang* men,
pulling dilapidated carts, hiding
what coins they pick up, have
thick bone joints—indestructible.

You know, at Dragon Boat Festival,
the strong fragrance of wormwood. We
stop where the cuckoo calls late night
to dawn from the shade of a far wood.
Your long eyelashes are closing. At hand,
a cool glass of water and the dying smoke
from ashes. Standing by the window,
I'm thinking: I love this world. There was
a moment, a time when I had my chance.
It glides slowly toward me, rounds the curve...

我总是这样。盯着荧屏，长久地
一行字跳出黑暗。黝黝的田野。矿灯飞快地向后
丘陵。水塘。夜晚从我的四肢碾过。
凄凉。单调。永不绝望
你知道，此时我低垂的额头亮起
一颗星：端着米钵。摇动铁轮的手臂
被活塞催起——火苗窜上来。一扇窗口
飘着晾晒的婴儿尿布，慢慢升高了……

真实

死人知道我们的谎言。在清晨
林间的鸟知道风。

果实知道大地之血的灌溉
哭声知道高脚杯的体面。

喉咙间的石头意味着亡灵在场
喝下它！猛兽的车轮需要它的润滑——

碾碎人，以及牙齿企图说出的真实。
世界在盲人脑袋的裂口里扭动

……黑暗从那里来

I'm always this way. Staring
forever at the computer screen.
A line of words jumping out
of the darkness. A black field. A miner's lamp
speeding backward. Hills. Ponds.
Deep night has rolled over my limbs.
Loneliness. Monotony. But never despair.
You know, at this moment, my head lowered,
a star shines on my brow. I'm carrying a rice bowl.
The piston-driven arm of clanging
iron wheels speeds up—tongues of flame
spurt out. Beyond this window, baby's
drying diapers flutter on the air. The star
slowly climbs...

TRUTH

The dead know our lies. At dawn,
birds in the forest know the wind.

Fruit knows the irrigation of this land with blood.
The voice crying knows the refined stem glass.

A stone in the throat means dead souls are with us.
Drink it up! Wheels of the beast need oiling—

crushing people and the truth that teeth try to speak.
In the opening in the skulls of the blind, the world twists

...from where does the darkness come

死亡之诗

……这时候我所向往的另一半是死亡
在故乡的天空下重新回到泥土
把最后一份财富分给贫穷的儿童
瘦弱的臂膊上搭着最后一名
双目失明的民歌手，走下水中
在背阴的山坡后面彻底消失
这时候我还能看到最后的
宝石之光、在静止不动的水面上……

1992，3，15

为大海而写的一支探戈

海风吹拂窗帘的静脉，天空的玫瑰
梦想打磨时光的镜片，我看见大海
的脚爪，在正午的镜子中倒立而出
把夏天的银器卷入狂暴的海水

你呵，你的孤独被大海侵犯，你梦中的鱼群
被大海驱赶。河流退向河汉

Xi Du

Xi Du is the pen name of Chen Guoping. He was born in Zhejiang Province in 1967 and received his BA in Chinese literature from Peking University in 1989. Since then he has been working at a publishing house in Beijing. Xi Du has published four books of poetry as well as two books of criticism.

Translated by Michelle Yeh

POEM OF DEATH

...At this moment the other half I long for is death
To return to the earth under the homeland sky
Give away the last of my fortune to the poor children
With the last balladeer, sightless, on my emaciated arm
I step into the river and disappear, once and for all
Behind the shady hill
At this hour I can still see the last
Gemlike glow, on the perfectly still water...

15 March 1992

A TANGO COMPOSED FOR THE OCEAN

A sea breeze brushes the veins of the window curtains; roses
In the sky dream of polishing the lenses of time. I see the ocean's
Talons rising upside down out of the mirror at high noon
To sweep summer's silver wares into the raging tide

Oh you, whose solitude is violated by the ocean that chases away
The school of fish in your dream. Rivers retreat to their tributaries

大海却从未把你放过，青铜铠甲的武士
海浪将你锻打，你头顶上绿火焰焚烧

而一面单数的旗帜被目击，离开复数的旗帜
在天空中独自展开，在一个人的头脑中
留下大海的芭蕾之舞，把脚尖踮起
你就会看见被蔑视的思想的高度

大海的乌贼释放出多疑的乌云
直升机降下暴雨闪亮的起落架
我阅读哲学的天空，诗歌的大海
一本书被放大到无限，押上波浪的韵脚

早上的暴风雨从海上带来
凉爽的气息，仍未从厨房的窗台上消失
在重要的时刻你不能出门，这是来自
暴风雨的告诫，和大海的愿望并不一致

通过上升的喷泉，海被传递到你的指尖
像马群一样狂野的海，飞奔中
被一根镀银的金属管勒住马头
黑铁的天空又倾倒出成吨的闪电

国家意志组织过奔腾的民意
夏天的大海却生了病。海水从街道上退去
暴露出成批蜂窝状的岩石和建筑
大海从树木退去，留下波浪的纹理

而星空选中在一个空虚的颅骨中飞翔
你打击一个人，就是抹去一片星空
帮助一个人，就是让思想得到生存的空间
当你从海滨抽身离去，一个夏天就此变得荒凉

1997，7，1

But the sea refuses to set you free. A tide of bronze-armored knights
Hammers you on the anvil; a green flame burns above your head

Witness the odd-numbered banner, set apart from
The even-numbered banners, unfurling alone in the sky
Leaving an imprint of the ocean ballet in someone's brain. If you
Stand on your toes, you can see how high disdained ideas are

Squids in the sea release dark clouds of suspicion
The helicopter lets down the storm's glistening landing gear
I read the philosophical sky, the ocean of poetry
A book expanding to infinity, in the rhyme of the waves

A morning storm brings crisp, cool air
From the ocean; it lingers on the windowsill in the kitchen
Don't go out at this critical moment. It is admonition
From the storm, at odds with the wishes of the sea

Through the rising water-fountain the ocean is transported
To your fingertips. The wild sea, like a galloping horse
Its head is jerked back by a silver-plated tube
The steely dark sky pours out tons of lightning again

Once, the will of the nation organized the surging will of the people
But the summer sea has fallen ill. Water recedes from the streets
Exposing the honeycombs of rocks and buildings
It retreats from the trees, leaving wavy patterns in its wake

Still the starry sky chooses to soar in an empty skull
To strike someone is to erase a piece of the starry sky
To help someone is to give thoughts space to stay alive
When you leave the beach, the entire summer turns desolate

1 July 1997

1967年

他们说：
"这把二胡的弦要扯断，
琴身要砸碎。"
我们就没有了琴声。

他们说：
"这棵大树要锯断，
主要是古树，全部要锯掉。"
我们就没有了阴凉。

他们说：
"这个石匠要除掉，
那个木匠也要除掉，要立即执行。"
我们就没有了好看的石桥，
我们就没有了好看的房子。

他们说：
"这些圣贤的书要烧掉，
这些文庙要毁掉，
这些出家人要赶回家。"
我们就没有了道德，
我们就没有了良知。

Yang Jian

Yang Jian was born in Taochong Mine, Fanchang County, Anhui Province, in 1967. He began writing poetry in the 1980s. A Buddhist at heart, he publicly follows Confucian precepts. He has published two collections of poetry.

Translated by Diana Shi
and George O'Connell

1967

They said
"Tear the strings from this erhu,
shatter that qin."
Thus we lost music.

They said
"Take this tall tree down,
and any that are old."
Thus we lost cool shade.

They said
"Get rid of this stonemason.
That carpenter too. Right now."
Thus no handsome stone bridges,
no stately homes.

They said
"Burn these sages' books.
Tear down these Confucian temples.
Drive out those monks and nuns."
Thus we have neither morals
nor conscience.

我生于崩溃的1967年，
我注定了要以毁灭的眼光来看待一切，
我生下来不久就生病了，
我注定了要以生病的眼光来看待一切。

看着你们都在死去，
我注定了不能死去，
我注定了要在废墟上开口说话，
我注定了要推开尘封的铁门。

2000

母羊和母牛

给庞培

1

有一年，
在山坡上，
我的心融化了，
在我的手掌上，
在我捏碎的一粒粒羊粪里。
那原来是田埂上的青草，
路边的青草。
我听见
自行车后架上
倒挂母羊的叫声，
就像一个小女孩
在喊：
"妈妈、妈妈……"
我的心融化了，
在空气里，
在人世上。

Born in the wreck of 1967,
I was doomed to see utter destruction.
Soon I fell ill,
my eyes knowing nothing but ruin.

Watching you all die,
I was destined not to,
my fate to speak from the rubble,
to throw the iron door sealed by dust wide open.

2000

NANNY GOATS, COWS

for Pang Pei

1

On the hillside one year
my heart dissolved,
in my palm
in the crumbling nuggets of goat dung
that was grass, green on the ridgeline,
green grass by the road.
I heard a nanny goat
slung head down
from the rack of a bicycle
calling like a girl,
"Mama, Mama..."
My heart dissolved
into the empty air,
into this human earth.

2

小时候，
乡村土墙上晒干的牛粪，
在火塘里燃烧着，
映红了母亲的脸。
我的心融化了，
那原来是田埂上的青草，
路边的青草。
现在我看见天上乌云翻滚，
暴雨倾注，
十头衰老的母牛过江，
犄角被麻绳
拴在车厢上。
它们的眼睛，
恭顺地望着雨水，
就像墙角边发青的土豆。
江水浩瀚、浑浊
冲向船帮，
在它们一动不动的眼前
溅起浪花。
快了，
呵，快到岸了，
那憨厚的十头母牛的眼睛，
那望着江水翻滚的
十头母牛的眼睛会去哪里？
我的心融化了，
在空气里，
在人世上。

2000

2

In the village of my childhood
cowshit dried on the mud walls,
then burned in the firepit,
Mother's face red and shining.
My heart dissolved.
All this was grass, green on the ridgeline,
green grass by the road.

Now I see dark clouds roll through the sky,
a torrent pouring down,
as ten old cows ferry the river,
horns roped to the truck rail,
watching the rain
through eyes meek as green potatoes in a corner.
The vast, turbid river
washes the hull,
surging, foaming
beneath their placid gaze.

Soon,
so soon ashore,
the eyes of ten simple, honest cows,
seeing the river roil,
ten cows' eyes, going where?
My heart dissolves
into the empty air,
into this human earth.

2000

雪的教育

"在东北这么多年，
没见过干净的雪。"
城市居民总这么沮丧。
在乡下，空地，或者森林的
树杈上，雪比矿泉水
更清洁，更有营养。
它甚至不是白的，而是
湛蓝，仿佛墨水瓶打翻
在熔炉里锻炼过一样
结实像石头，柔美像模特。
在空中的T形台上
招摇，而在山阴，它们
又比午睡的猫更安静。
风的爪子调皮地在它的脸上
留下细的纹路，它连一个身
也不会翻。而是静静地
搂着怀里的草芽

Sang Ke

Sang Ke was born in Heilongjiang Province in 1967. He graduated from the Beijing Normal University Chinese literature department in 1989 and currently lives in Harbin. He has published a number of poetry collections, and his works have been translated into many languages. He has also published translations of Larkin's selected poems and Auden's *Academic Graffiti*. Sang's poetry has received the Liu Li-an Poetry Prize and The Peoples' Literature Poetry Prize.

Translated by Jane Weizhen Pan
and Martin Merz

ENLIGHTENED BY SNOW

"In all my years in Manchuria,
I never saw pristine snow."
City folk are always despondent.
In the countryside, out in open spaces, or
on forks of boughs in the forest,
snow is more pristine, more nourishing
than mineral water.
That snow isn't white, but sky blue.
Rock hard, like spilled blue ink annealed in a crucible.
Supple, like a fashion model swaying down a catwalk in the air.
But in the shade of a mountain,
more tranquil than a napping cat.
The wind's claws are mischievous,
leaving fine lines on its face, but no,
snow doesn't budge.
It quietly cradles grass sprouts,

或者我们童年时代
的记忆和几近失传的游戏。
在国防公路上，它被挤压
仿佛轮胎的模块儿。
把它的嘎吱声理解成呻吟
是荒谬的。它实际上
更像一种对强制的反抗。
而我，嘟嘟囔囔，也
正有这个意思。如果
这还算一种功绩，那是因为
我始终在雪仁慈的教育下。

1999，11，21

我的拇指

1

我的拇指不在了
我的拇指它死了
你可以认为它是被菜刀切去了
你可以认为它是被刺刀切去了
它长在食指的右边，这是左手
它长在食指的左边，这是右手
我的手盖着一篇文章
关于自由，关于权利
关于我的拇指明明长着
我却瞪大眼睛说它不在

2

我的拇指去过五个朝代
我的拇指去过九个省份
我知道关于时间我说对了一半
我知道关于地点我说错了一半
我知道我是处女地

or our childhood memories
and long-forgotten games.
Tire treads squish snow on highways.
How absurd to mistake that crunching sound for moaning.
It is in fact
more like a revolt against coercion.
And so is my muffled mumbling.
If this can be called an achievement,
it is thanks to the enlightenment of the merciful snow.

21 November 1999

MY THUMBS

1

My thumbs are gone
My thumbs are dead
You may say, chopped off with a cleaver
Or cleaved away with a bayonet
It was to the right of my index finger
—That's my left hand
It was to the left of my index finger
—That's my right hand
My hands hide an essay
About freedom, about rights
About the existence of my thumbs
While I profess they're gone

2

My thumbs have been to five dynasties
My thumbs have been to nine provinces
I know I'm half right about the time
I know I'm half wrong about the place
I know I am virgin soil

我知道我是小戏子
我的心田朝廷的铁犁没有耕耘
我的台词班主的钢鞭没有光临
我把我思想的处女膜捅破了
我把我塑造的角色推下山崖

3
你看见我的拇指是怎么长大的
你看见我的拇指和食指的恋爱
它和中指的奸情让手羞愧
它和小指的友谊让手叹惋
我和我的拇指隔着一座高山
我和我的拇指隔着一片大海
如果立场的高山崩塌
如果策略的大海枯干
我和我的拇指将无话可谈
我和我的拇指将惺惺相怜

4
但是我啃秃了我的拇指的指甲
但是我扯掉了我的拇指的披肩
指甲啊是真实的甲胄
披肩啊是比喻的皮肉
我知道我的拇指的疼痛
我知道我的拇指的狂欢
它疼了它的神经战栗仿佛敏感的亚麻
它乐了它的快感来临仿佛神秘的大麻
亚麻茁壮地成长
大麻转移到地下

2001，3，17

I know I am a mere opera performer
My heart is free of the plow of power
My actor's lines are free of my teacher's whip
I break the hymen of my mind
I push the role I created off a cliff

3
You saw how my thumbs grew up
You saw their romance with my index fingers
Their philandering with my ring fingers shamed my hands
Their friendships with my little fingers saddened my hands
A mountain separates my thumbs and me
An ocean separates my thumbs and me
If the mountain of principles crumbles
If the sea of strategy evaporates
My thumbs and I will have nothing to say to each other
My thumbs and I will pity one another

4
But I have gnawed away my thumbnails
But I have torn away my thumbs' capes
The nails were real armor
The capes are my analogy for skin
I know my thumbs' pain
I know my thumbs' revelry
They are in pain they shudder like sensitive flax
They are ecstatic they quiver like mysterious hemp
Flax grows with vigor
Hemp goes underground

17 March 2001

前世

要逃，就干脆逃到蝴蝶的体内去
不必再咬着牙，打翻父母的阴谋和药汁
不必等到血都吐尽了。
要为敌，就干脆与整个人类为敌。
他哗地一下脱掉了蘸墨的青袍
脱掉了一层皮
脱掉了内心朝飞暮倦的长亭短亭。
脱掉了云和水
这情节确实令人震悚：他如此轻易地
又脱掉了自己的骨头！
我无限眷恋的最后一幕是：他纵身一跃
在枝头等了亿年的蝴蝶浑身一颤
暗叫道：来了！
这一夜明月低于屋檐
碧溪潮生两岸

只有一句尚未忘记
她忍住百感交集的泪水

Chen Xianfa

Chen Xianfa was born in October 1967 in Tongcheng, Anhui Province. He graduated from Fudan University in 1989. His publications include two books of poetry and a novel. His works have appeared in English, French, Russian, and Spanish translations. Chen was highly commended as "a poet who has most perfectly assimilated the essence of Chinese culture and the modernist aesthetics," and was named one of the ten major burgeoning poets in China 1986–2006.

Translated by Lisa Lai-ming Wong

THE PREVIOUS LIFE

To cut and run, head straight into the butterfly's body
No more teeth-clenching, spoiling the parents' plot and potion
No more waiting until the last drop of blood is disgorged
To oppose, then be an opponent to all humankind
Whoosh! In a split second he sloughs the ink-stained scholarly robe
Sloughs a layer of skin
Sloughs from the heart those flutters of fond meetings and partings
Sloughs the cloud and water
Indeed, this is a stunning episode: with such ease he
Sloughs his bones too!
It is the final scene that I always yearn for: off he goes in one leap
In one shudder the butterfly, having waited on the bough over the eons
Whispers: There he is
This night the bright moon sinks below the eaves
The tide rises at the banks of the emerald stream

Only one line stays in the mind
She holds back her tears of myriad emotions

把左翅朝下压了压，往前一伸
说：梁兄，请了
请了——

2004，6，2

秩序的顶点

在狱中我愉快地练习倒立。
我倒立，群山随之倒立
铁栅间狱卒的脸晃动
远处的猛虎
也不得不倒立。整整一个秋季
我看着它深深的喉咙

2005，9

Her left wing gently presses, and stretches forward
She says, Farewell, dear brother Liang
Farewell

2 June 2004

THE ULTIMATE ORDER

In jail I joyfully practice headstands
When I do a headstand, the mountains do their headstands, too
Between the iron bars the jailer's face wavers
At the far end the fierce tiger
Cannot help but do a headstand. Throughout autumn
I have been watching its fathomless throat

September 2005

韩熙载夜宴图

雪下了整整一夜，你猛然醒了。
窗外，漆黑，犹如往常。雨后，
几声虫鸣将树林点缀成薄雾轻起的江面。
你又睡下了，雪继续在下，铺天盖地。

睡梦中有人叫你起床，看日出。
雪中看日出？疑问的微风轻轻拂面。
但你还是起床，跟在那人身后——
跨进九曲回廊的院落，有人啼哭。

寻着哭声，树影在灯下摇晃。
书影里，铁骑和人群如昨夜的风雪
卷过街市。禁令一个接着一个颁布——
雪白的天地间，渐渐血流成河。

打开窗户，雨势见小，心跳渐慢。
黄酒里歌声不断，落叶高高飘扬。
风卷白云，拉坯的姐弟合衣相拥而眠，
酣声如雨。梦里，他们看天下雪，

Lin Mu

Lin Mu was born in 1967 and began writing poetry in 1986. His poetry has been in a variety of anthologies and literary magazines. Most of his work appears in self-published collections.

Translated by Julie Chiu

THE NIGHT REVELS OF HAN XIZAI, A HANDSCROLL

Snowing all night. You wake up with a start.
Outside the window. Pitch-black. Like always. After the rain,
a few notes of insect songs decorate the wood, like thin mist rising
      from the river.
You drift back to sleep. Snow continues to fall, filling earth and sky.

In your dream a voice is calling, Get up, let's see the sunrise.
See the sunrise in the snow? A breeze gently brushes the cheek, puzzled.
Still, you get up and follow that person—
into a courtyard, a corridor with nine turns. Someone's crying.

You go in search of the crying, shadows of trees sway in the lamp.
Shadows of books, where armored cavalry and crowds sweep across the
      market
like last night's snowstorm. Come the bans, one after another—
in the white between earth and sky, blood gathers into a river.

You open the window. Rain's died down. Heartbeat's eased up.
Rice wine induces endless singing. Fallen leaves drift on high.
Wind swirls the white clouds, sister and brother, cuddled up in the
      same garb, sleep on—
two potter kids whose snores fall like rain. They watch the snowfall in
      their dream,

看自己唱歌，看一群人表演拍胸脯。
都是浪尖上讨生活，双眉紧锁不如放浪形骸。
山空人黑，水流花开，小心吓着。
天色尚早，硝烟未散，再睡一会儿吧。*

2007，07，06

---

*韩熙载夜宴图：五代画家顾闳中作，原作已佚失，今版本为宋人摹本。此图绢本设色，宽28.7厘米，长335.5厘米，现藏北京故宫博物院。

关于《韩熙载夜宴图》的绘制背景，《宣和画谱》中这样记载："是时中书舍人韩熙载，以贵游世胄，多好声伎，专为夜饮，虽宾客揉杂，欢呼狂逸，不复拘制，李氏惜其才，置而不问。声传中外，颇闻其荒纵，然欲见樽俎灯烛间觥筹交错之态度不可得，乃命闳中夜至其第窃窥之，目识心记，图绘以上之，故世有夜宴图。"但南唐后主李煜又觉命人"写臣下私亵以观"有失体统，应"阅而弃之"。可是，此图还是入了北宋御府画库。

watch themselves sing, watch people give a show of chest-beating.
All to make a living riding the waves, so why not let the hair down
      but frown?
Hills are empty, figures are dark. Flowers bloom as water flows on. Just
      don't be scared.
It's still early, and the gunfire hasn't ceased. Might as well sleep
      some more.*

6 July 2007

———————

* Poet's note: *The Night Revels of Han Xizai* was a painting by Gu Hong-
zhong of the Five Dynasties (907–960). The original now lost, the ex-
tant painting is an imitation made in the Song dynasty (960–1279).
Presently kept in the Palace Museum in Beijing, the Song copy is
painted in colors on a silk scroll, measuring 28.7 cm vertically and
335.5 cm across.

    The background of the original painting is thus recorded in the
Xuanhe huapu (The Xuanhe painting catalogue): "Han Xizai, an offi-
cial of the imperial secretariat, loved to befriend aristocrats and en-
tertain himself with song girls. He often hosted drinking parties in
the night. His guests were rowdy and rough, cheering and acting
wildly at his parties. Han did not try to restrain them. Emperor Li
loved Han for his talents, and let him be. Word about Han's dissolute
life spread far and wide. The emperor heard about it, and was eager
to know how Han conducted himself as wine vessels and chips lay
scattered about meat blocks, jars, and lamps. He therefore ordered
Gu Hongzhong to pay a visit to Han's residence and spy on the party.
Gu committed to memory whatever met his eyes, and depicted the
details in a painting for the emperor. *The Night Revels of Han Xizai* was
thus made." Yet Emperor Li felt it not decorous that he order some-
one to "paint a subordinate's private life for his eyes," and believed
that he should "take a look and then be rid of it." Still, the painting
found its way into the imperial painting library of the Northern Song
dynasty (960–1127).

平沙落雁图

吃我一刀。睡梦中，你劈头盖脸
向那人挥刀砍去。角落里，
尘土飞扬。转眼间那人灰飞烟灭。
好梦，好梦！睡梦中，你大呼小叫，
仿佛得了失心疯。你面含喜色，
安然睡去。这一睡就是一十八年。
十八年后，我病怏怏来到这人世间。
睡梦中，时常被一只鸟儿吓醒。
睡梦中，你用同一只鸟安慰我。
笛声悠扬，流水潺潺。隔海眺望，
天水澹澹，烟雾中，突然大雪纷飞。
雪后，山市晴岚，一片白帆
自远处悠然荡来。夕阳中，两人
正举杯对饮。那情形仿佛八百年前，
一船小和尚，只剩下船夫一人，
没有川资，便将自己献给万里波涛。
一波才动万波随。哦满船明月
映着你的笑脸，一张熟睡的笑脸。
睡梦中，你化作一只鸟飞回家。
睡梦中，我手起刀落。手起刀落。
嗨！风雨里的机趣与平和。风雨中，
一只牛和一只熊，打得正欢。
风雨中，我们俩佯装惊诧，疯癫癫
加入嬉闹的行列。风停雨歇，

WILD GEESE ALIGHT ON SANDY BAR

Take this! In the dream, targeting some scalp and face
you raise your knife and hack. There in that corner,
a dance of dirt and dust. Blink, and the man's no more.
Hell of a good dream!—In the dream, you yell out
like you've totally lost your mind. Your face beams with joy,
you peacefully fall asleep. Sleep that lasts eighteen years.
Eighteen years later, I come to the human world, sickly.
In the dream, I am often startled by a bird.
In the dream, you comfort me with the same bird.
Notes of a melodious flute. Murmurs of a swift stream. A gaze down
     the distant sea,
water and sky, one quietude. Mist gathers, and suddenly a heavy snow.
After the snow, sun shines on the hill town, afloat in haze. A white sail
drifts in from afar, leisurely swaying. As the sun sets, two drinkers
raise their cups in a toast. As if it's eight hundred years back
when on board a boat full of young monks, the boatman alone
is short of fares for the journey, so he gives himself to the endless waves.
One wave moves and thousands follow. Moonlight fills the boat and
shines on your smiling face, a face deep in sleep and smiling.
In the dream, you become a bird, winging your way home.
In the dream, I raise my arm and hack. Raise my arm and hack.
Ah, the joy of chance, the peace in wind and rain. In wind and rain
an ox and a bear are at the height of their fighting.
In wind and rain, we feign surprise. Mad-eyed and blighted,
we join the rowdy revelers. The wind dies down. The rain stops.

只见满地的落叶，满地的蹄印脚印。
满天飞舞着，雪白的纸钱，和酒香。*

2007，08，29

孤鸟图轴

一只乾隆镂花小碗，它，仿佛一只鸟
立在我的心头，颤巍巍，站在心尖尖上。
随着心跳的起伏，它一会儿展翅高飞，一会儿
沉入谷底，和着大气环流，四处觅食，四处抢食，
四处厮打，四处留情、交媾、孵小鸟。
当然，它也有休息的时候，它鼾声如雷，
旁若无人。今天，它就是一首诗，处理着我，
和它之间纠缠不休也纠缠不清的关系。
一只碗，三分利。如果我把它扩大，
放在祖国的庞大天平上，它是一只老虎，
一只变色虎，今天一身金黄，明天一脸碧绿。
饥饿这个词总折磨它，纠缠它，淬炼它。
利益均分，它喜欢这个词，利用它制定丛林法则。
丛林需要法则，以便更好地保护蜗牛、蚂蚁和老鼠。
大象有点不高兴，它的利益被忽略了；
北极熊很生气、很暴躁，一掌拍碎螃蟹的前爪。

风云密布，气氛紧张，老虎悄悄撒了泡尿。
越是危险，利益越发重要。"都想吃饱吃好，

---

* 平沙落雁，潇湘八景之一。潇湘八景，中国艺术史上的著名画题，为北宋宋迪
所创，分别是：山市晴岚、远浦归帆、平沙落雁、潇湘夜雨、烟寺晚钟、渔村
夕照、江天暮色、洞庭秋月。此后，诸多画家都以此为画题作画，以追求平和
淡雅的审美风格，慢慢演变成中国画中一个固定画题，进而影响到诗歌和音
乐。南宋画家法常画有《潇湘八景图》，后流入日本，并影响了日本绘画和园
林艺术；元代作家马致远曾以"潇湘八景"写过八支曲子。

Fallen leaves everywhere. Everywhere, hoofprints and footprints.
In the air, a dance: paper offerings white as snow, the aroma of wine.*

29 August 2007

LONE BIRD: A VERTICAL SCROLL

A porcelain bowl of the Qianlong era, smallish and engraved, is like
    a bird
standing atop my heart, wobbly, it perches on the tip of my heart
rising and falling with the heartbeat, winging high, sinking low
in the valley's depth. Following the atmospheric circular flow, it hunts,
    snatches,
scuffles everywhere, here and there loving, mating, hatching birds.
Surely there's a time for rest, too, and it snores like thunder
as if there's it and it alone. Today, it is a poem, sorting out
our ever-enmeshed never-unraveled entanglement.

One single bowl, three measures of profit. If we enlarge it
and place it on the giant scale of our fatherland, it's a tiger,

---

* Poet's note: *Wild Geese Alight on Sandy Bar* is one of the eight themes in
the Eight Views of the Xiao and Xiang, a famous motif in the history
of Chinese art. It was first created by Song Di of the Northern Song
dynasty (960–1127). The eight views, realized as eight paintings in a
series, are: Sunlight on Hill Town in Haze, Homecoming Sails at Dis-
tant Shore, Wild Geese Alight on Sandy Bar, Night Rain on the Xiao
and Xiang, Evening Bell at Mist-Shrouded Temple, Fishing Village
in Sunset Glow, Sky and River at Dusk, and Autumn Moon over Lake
Dongting. Since its first creation, many painters have taken up the
motif. With an aesthetics of tranquillity and subdued elegance, it
has gradually become a fixed motif in Chinese painting and has ex-
tended its influence to poetry and music. Many artists of the South-
ern Song painted works entitled *The Eight Views of the Xiao and Xiang*,
and the motif subsequently spread its influence to Japanese painting
and landscape gardening. In the Yuan dynasty (1271–1368), Ma Zhi-
yuan composed eight musical pieces under the title of "Eight Views
of the Xiao and Xiang."

没门！"老虎发威了。"谁敢打砸抢，
狐狸就咬断谁的小鸡鸡；谁敢哄抬物价、制造混乱，
小心你们的老婆被猪卖给人贩子，先奸后杀！"
老虎语无伦次，一着急就现出了人形。
一群猴子用狂吠掩饰心中的喜悦，野鸡和鸭低低哀鸣。
一个俯冲，小鸟撞碎青花，溅我一脸釉彩。*

2008，04，06

---

* 孤鸟图轴，八大山人(朱耷)晚年作品，现藏云南省博物馆。这副立轴，从画的
左侧底部斜斜地向上伸出一根虬枝，枝尖立着一只小鸟，很是夺目。虬枝孤
鸟，画家似乎想告诉我们，这个世界是孤独的，也是危险的，但危机四伏中又
透着某种安宁的气息。瞧，那只鸟的眼睛，那根孤立无依的虬枝对它来说并不
危险，那是它生活的常态。在这根树枝上它获得了足够的休息，或正将休息。
　　三百多年来，八大山人以他的孤傲名世，他装聋作哑不与人语，似乎在用自
己的生命证悟——"一口吸进西江水"的洪州禅理。
　　八大山人的诗、书、画、印章、别号，相互映照，从不同侧面和角度折射他
孜孜以求的"平等一禅心"。在他心里，没有贪念，没有嘲讽，没有争斗，也
没有禅机，只有天心、童趣和幽默，以及对世间万物的厚爱。
　　八大山人的时代与今天别无区别。在各种利益和妄念面前，这个世界反而显
得孤独无助，但在洪荒宇宙中这个世界又仿佛是那只看似孤立无援的鸟，闲来
无事就笑看利益一边充当正义的面具，一边扮演政治的灵魂。

a camouflage tiger, all-over gold today, emerald in the face tomorrow.

The word *hunger* often torments it, nags it, tempers it.

Even division of profits—it likes this one, and lays down jungle rules
      with it.

The jungle needs rules to better protect the snail, the ant, the rat.

Elephant isn't so happy, for its interests are overlooked.

Polar Bear's quite angry; agitated, it crashes the crab's front legs with
      its paw.

Storm clouds gather. The air is tense. Tiger secretly takes a piss.

The greater the danger, the more profits matter. "All wanna be fed nice
      and good?

No way!" So Tiger gets rough. "Whoever dares beat smash loot,

his thingy'll be chewed off by the fox. Try price-gouging and fomenting
      chaos,

the pig'll sell your wife to the man-trafficker, get her raped and
      butchered!"

Talking nonsense, getting all anxious, Tiger shows its human form.

Monkeys let out wild gibbers to cover up their joy, wild chicks and
      ducks, plaintive, softly cluck and quack.

With a quick dive, the bird smashes the bowl, and splashes glaze all
      over my face.*

6 April 2008

------

* Poet's note: *Lone Bird: A Vertical Scroll* is a work Bada Shanren painted
in his later years. (Literally, *ba* means "eight" [of the eighth genera-
tion], *da* means "big" [with big ears], and *shanren* means "man of the
mountains.") The scroll is presently housed in the Museum of Yun-
nan Province. In this vertical scroll, a crooked, knotty branch ex-
tends from the bottom left and cuts across the scroll, on top of which
perches a little bird, a very eye-catching scene. A lone bird atop a
crooked branch. The painter seems to want to tell us that the world
is a lonely place, a dangerous place, but where danger lurks a certain
peace also permeates. Behold the eye of the bird. For it, the helpless,
lone branch is no danger—it is but a regular mode of existence. On
this very branch the bird has taken a good rest, or will take a good rest.

For three hundred years, Bada Shanren has been known for his solitude and pride. He pretended to be deaf and dumb and would not talk to anybody. It was as if he were meditating, with his whole being, on the Zen Buddhist teaching from Hongzhou: "Take in the West River with a sip."

Bada Shanren's poetry, calligraphy, paintings, seal engravings, and alias (he was born Zhu Da and only adopted the name Bada Shanren in his later years) illuminate one another, depicting from different angles and in different profiles the "mind of equanimity and one Zen," which he keenly sought. In the heart of Bada Shanren, there was no greed, no sarcasm, no conflicts, no Zen, only the mind of heaven, the fun of a child, a sense of humor, and a deep love for the multiplicities of the world.

Bada Shanren's era is no different from ours. In the face of benefits and ambition, the present world is but lonely and hapless. Placed in the primordial universe, this world is like the helpless lone bird painted by Bada Shanren, which in its leisure contemplates interests and profits with a smile, how they become justice's mask while playing the soul of politics.

翼

有着旗帜的形状，但她们
从不沉迷于随风飘舞
她们的节拍器（谁的发明？）
似乎专门用来抗拒风的方向
显然，她们有自己隐秘的目标。
当她们长在我们躯体的暗处
（哦，去他的风车的张扬癖！）
她们要用有形的弧度，对称出
飞禽与走兽的差别
（天使和蝙蝠不包括于其中）
假如她们的意志发展成一项
事业，好像飞行也是
一种生活或维持生活的手段
她们会意识到平衡的必要
但所有的旗帜都不在乎
这一点；而风筝
安享于摇头摆尾的快乐。
当羽翼丰满，躯体就会感到
一种轻逸，如同正从内部
鼓起了一个球形的浮漂

Zhou Zan

Zhou Zan, a native of Jiangsu Province, was born in 1968. She has worked as a poet, scholar, and translator. From 2006 to 2007 she was a visiting scholar at Columbia University in New York City. Editor of the women's poetry journal *Wings,* she has published one book of poetry and two collections of poetry criticism. She has translated a selection of poetry by the Canadian writer Margaret Atwood.

Translated by Steve Riep

WINGS

though shaped like banners, the women
never indulge in dancing in the wind,
their metronome (who invented it?)
seems to be set mainly to resist the wind's direction,
obviously they have their own, hidden objective.
When they grow in the hidden parts of our bodies
(oh, that blasted windmill's weakness for public spectacle!)
they must use a curved form, to bring out symmetrically
the difference between the birds and the beasts
(not including angels and bats);
if their will develops into a
cause, like flying also is
a way of living or a means of supporting life,
they will realize the need for balance,
but not a single banner cares the least about
this point, and kites
content themselves with complacent happiness.
When wings are full, the bodies will feel
a kind of ease and freedom, like a ball-shaped buoy
that comes from within and swells outward;

因而，一条游鱼的羽翅
决非退化的小摆设，它仅意味着
心的自由必须对称于水的流动

2000，6，7

匠人

他曾拜名师，使用模具
他使技艺娴熟，留下过样品
又被另一幅杰作覆盖
师长们的夸赞，客户抢购
如今他离开众人
一心一意，陷入沉思
他随意拿起一块石头雕刻
期待中一个生命诞生
有一个形体，也许并不优美
也许能开口说话，也许保持沉静

她可能一直是摸索，从第一根绳线开始
她捡起来，编织，她纠缠
联系，没有师父，没有样本
当她渐渐从线团中找到结合
和网络的方向，她知道
生命已经开始，她漫不经心
用最快乐的感情
也许她因这创造而闻名，也许她永远隐姓

2005，6，19

thus, the fins of a swimming fish
are by no means retrogressive ornaments, but merely imply that
the heart's freedom must be symmetrical to the flow of the water.

7 June 2000

ARTISANS

He once studied under a famous master and used molds;
he honed his skill to perfection and left samples of his work,
one masterpiece covering the next
that teachers praised, customers rushed to purchase.
Now he has left everyone behind,
and lost in thought, with all his heart and soul
he takes up a piece of stone to sculpt as he pleases;
as he waits, a new life is born;
it has form, but perhaps is in no way graceful,
maybe it can open its mouth and speak, or maybe it will just keep silent.

Maybe she has been groping all along, starting from the very first thread;
she takes it up, weaves it, tangles it,
and connects it in, without master or pattern,
but gradually from within this web of threads she finds things coming
        together
and a direction to her network of threads emerges; she realizes
that life has already begun, and carelessly
employs her happiest feeling—
maybe her creation will make her famous, or maybe she will never
        be known.

19 June 2005

练习曲

立秋后依然如此闷热，
从邻近那幢楼里传来的练习曲
比连日的低气压更像一场折磨。
那个瘦瘦的、扎着马尾辫的小姑娘，
每天都在窗边反复地弹奏，琴声
就像一盒坏损的旧磁带卡在录音机中。

我熟悉这尖厉的旋律，
以每只高悬在电线杆上的大喇叭，
它们曾经垄断童年的天空，
辐射无处不在，即使我捂上耳朵，
也能听见标语像歌词，像握紧的拳头，
在墙壁上一遍遍地怒吼……

或许这就是我难以爱音乐的原因，
我更爱沉默，受虐的后遗症。
因为在听觉的全部记忆里，
只有一种气候和一种C调的轰鸣——
我更爱那些静静摆放的乐器，
当它们不被弹奏时，会在微光中闪亮着童贞。

Zhu Zhu

Zhu Zhu, a poet, essayist, and art critic, was born in 1969. He lives in Nanjing. He has published a number of volumes of poetry, and his work has been translated into English, French, Italian, and Japanese. He has been the recipient of several prizes, including *Shanghai Literature*'s annual prize for poetry in 2000.

Translated by Jennifer Feeley

ÉTUDE

Early autumn, yet still sweltering.
The étude intruding from a neighboring building
torments more than the endless low pressure systems.
A skinny, ponytailed girl
practices daily beside the window, the din of the piano
like a cassette deck jammed with an old, broken tape.

I recognize the deafening melody
that once conspired with loudspeakers perched high on utility poles
to monopolize my childhood sky.
It radiated everywhere; even if I covered my ears,
the rallying lyrics persisted, like clenched fists
beating against walls over and over again...

Perhaps that's why I can't appreciate music:
I prefer silence in the aftermath of torment.
In my entire auditory memory,
I can only recall one particular climate and one type of rumbling C note—
Maybe I prefer instruments that are laid out and remain quiet:
when they're not being played, they chastely glimmer in the dim light.

如今我以为，至少耳朵已不在炼狱里生活，
在垂放着百叶窗的家中，噪音
只来自洗衣机的滚筒声和低弱的车流，
当我抬头望向郊外的山脉，会庆幸
自己就像小木桶里未刷成标语的石灰，
转而在涂写可能的自由——

然而，沿着这小姑娘的指尖
那些被埋葬的音符如同幽灵
纷纷地复活，如同电影里
一辆辆满载士兵的卡车，
或者，如同恐怖小说中的病毒，
通过声波将瘟疫重新扩散在全城。

哦，多么邪恶而聪明的设计，将
这样的曲子编进一本入门的琴谱里，
哦，无辜的小姑娘，沉浸在勤奋的练习中，
梦想能成为音乐家，有一天坐在舞台上，
从聚光灯的下方撑起黑色的琴盖，
却全然不知自己是打开了盒子的潘多娜。

海岛

有牛孰不在岛上？

苏轼

放逐，这就是对权力说真话的结果，
但也不必过于美化他，将他的政治头脑
看得和他的诗人头脑一样发达，
给他一个国家，他终究不脱独裁的臼窠。

现在他已抵达了这个国家的南极，
或者是抵达了若干个世纪之后的今天
一个诗人的位置：被彻底地边缘化，
好像黄昏时空荡的海滨浴场上

Now it seems at least my ears are free from purgatory;
in a home hung with window blinds, the noise
comes from faint traffic and the hum of a washing machine.
When I look up at outlying mountain chains, I rejoice that I'm
like a bucket of lime not made to paint slogans,
instead used to scrawl freedom's possibilities—

And yet, beneath this girl's fingertips,
buried musical notes become spirits
revived key by key, or a truck
packed with soldiers as in a movie,
or like a virus in a horror novel
where sound waves again propagate a citywide plague.

Oh, what a dark and cunning design, compiling
such tunes into elementary sheet music.
Oh, innocent girl, engrossed in daily lessons,
dreaming of becoming a virtuoso: one day sitting on stage,
black piano lid propped up beneath the spotlight,
no clue that she is Pandora and has uncovered the box.

ISLAND

> *During one's lifetime, who does not live on an island?*
> SU SHI (1037-1101)

Exile, the outcome of speaking the truth in the face of authority—
but there's no need to glamorize him, nor contend that his political mind
is as advanced as his poetic one.
Give him a country, and he'll fall into the trap of a despot.

Now he's landed in the country's southern extreme,
or maybe in the present after centuries have passed.
A poet's position: to be marginalized,
like a deserted beach at dusk,

被遗留在桌上的收音机。大陆
像收起了吊桥的城市远在海的另一边，
群山般环抱的潮水，退去如雪崩般
无情，只留下泡沫、珊瑚和成堆的垃圾。

他栽种竹子如同戍边的将士带来了
情人的照片，在米酒中酿造江南，
他读陶渊明，在这里读就像有
一架天文望远镜猛然将猎户星推入心扉。

小路在村外连接起荒寂，贫乏，瘴疠。
酷热，足以烧熔棚顶和心智。
唯有月亮感恩于他不朽的赞颂，
频频来访，在长夜里治疗他的失忆。

噢，他必须收起鲁宾逊的傲慢，
在异化的环境里重新定调。
他必须振作精神，不扮演文明的遗老，
不做词语的幽灵，不卖弄苦难，

而只是澄清生命的原址——
以它为一种比例尺，重新丈量大陆，
绘下新的世界地图，或者
像沙鸥一无所负，自在地滑翔。

or a radio forgotten on the table. The mainland
is a city with a raised drawbridge, tucked at the far edge of the sea;
the tide encloses like a mountain range, retreats as if an avalanche,
ruthless, leaving behind only foam, coral, and banks of trash.

He cultivates bamboo the way a frontier soldier clutches
his beloved's photograph. Rice wine conjures up memories of Jiangnan
and reading Tao Yuanming. Reading here feels like
a telescope that has suddenly thrust Orion into the window of his heart.

The path outside the village connects loneliness, poverty, and disease.
It's scorching, hot enough to melt shed covers and intelligence.
Only the moon pays attention to his enduring eulogies,
calling on him night after endless night to cure his amnesia.

Oh, what he must do is shed his Robinson Crusoe arrogance
and start afresh in these foreign surroundings.
He needs to man up, stop playing the castaway of a lost civilization,
avoid vanishing into a mere specter of words, can the self-pity.

All this only serves to chart his life's original compass point,
a scale to remeasure the mainland
and sketch a new world map. The other option is to just
let it all go, like a seagull without a single care, and glide freely.

古猿部落

树林里落满果实，猩红的地毯
源于地质的变迁
水退了，老虎的剑齿烂了
我们围着空地商量未来
老的刚从进化里爬出，挥老拳
少的已按耐不住舌头，要第一个
去吃梅花鹿，移山的志向没有
倒可以涉水，南方北方的
田野只是一张餐桌
所谓共和闹哄哄
还是独裁之秋赶走蚊蝇
好在我们都直立着
可以观天象，徒手挣脱了食物链
但十月的劳动力
还是倾向剩余：不需要画皮，烹饪
肉身当木柴，只有公的继续
将母的掀翻，朗诵它的美
但要说出"我爱你"
至少春花秋月的，还要两百万年

Jiang Tao

Jiang Tao was born in 1970 in Tianjin. Educated at Tsinghua and Peking Universities, he is currently an associate professor in the Chinese department at Peking University. He began to write poetry in the early 1990s, and he conducts research on modern literature and culture. Jiang Tao's publications include a poetry collection and a monograph.

Translated by Allan H. Barr

PRIMATE TRIBE

Fruit litters the forest, a scarlet carpet
Laid by geology's vicissitudes
The waters receded, the tiger's saber-tooth rotted
Round a circle in the clearing we ponder the future
The elders clambering out of evolution swing their old fists
The youngsters with restless tongues eager to be first
To eat a sika deer, we do not hanker to move mountains
But fording streams comes easy, north and south
The wilderness is one big dining table
Our so-called republic a riotous din
Before dictatorial autumn chased away the mosquitoes and flies
The good thing is now we stand up straight
To stargaze, the food chain thrown off bare-handed
But October's labor force
Still tends toward a surplus: no need to mask or cook
And bodies serve as kindling when the male keeps on
Pinning his mate to the ground, reciting her allure
But to say "I love you"—
At least with spring-and-autumn charm—
    will take another two million years

2007致麦小克：良人

我死的时候
蚂蚁带着搬运队过来，它们商量
收割我的哪个部分
最好的是我的心脏
生猛，食肉动物，宜红烧，亦可清蒸
我嘴角的弧度
代表一个人愉快的白天与黑夜
尚有些零碎事件
分别属于我的肝脏，肺，膀胱和下水
我的子宫是一片上好的墓地
风水纯良，孩儿们嬉戏，三十年河东三十年河西
而我的舌头是一座火山，覆盖冰雪
和石头交换过火焰

快死的时候我坐在空荡荡的门槛
等待有人检查我的牙齿
最后一次
掏出我最孤独的部分：我的来生
它将把我的灵魂带到别处去旅行

2006，12

Yan Wo

Yan Wo, an ethnic Hakka, was born in 1970. She went online in 1998 and has been involved in a variety of web-based poetry activities. She published her first collection in 2006. The following year she served as a juror for poetry competitions and began working in poetry criticism. She makes her home in Guangzhou.

Translated by John A. Crespi

TO MY HUSBAND, MAI XIAOKE, IN 2007

As I die
the ants bring their moving crew. They confer
on what parts of me to harvest.
Best of all is my heart:
fresh meat from a carnivore: ideal for braising, or steaming.
The arc of my lips
signifies days and nights of pleasure.
And there are those little incidents
that belong respectively to my liver, lungs, bladder, and intestines.
My uterus makes a fine cemetery.
The feng shui is excellent   children frolic   fortunes rise and fall.
My tongue is a snowcapped volcano
that has traded flame with stones.

I sit on a bare doorsill as death nears,
waiting for someone to examine my teeth
and for the last time extract
that loneliest part of me, my next life,
so my soul may journey elsewhere.

December 2006

又赠大碗

让男孩慢下来
成为父亲
让女孩也慢下来
成为母亲
金色的田野上
稻草人结着草籽
每一颗都是父亲母亲
它们笑起来
喜悦挠过母麻雀的小肚皮

2008

THE GIFT OF ANOTHER BIG BOWL

Slow the boys down
   to become fathers.
And slow the girls down
   to become mothers.
In a field of gold
   straw men bear grass seed,
   every seed a father, a mother.
The straw men smile.
Joy rubs gently past a mother sparrow's belly.

2008

海的形状

你每次问我海的形状时，
我都应该拎回两袋海水。
这是海的形状，像一对眼睛；
或者是眼睛看到的海的形状。
你去摸它，像是去擦拭
两滴滚烫的眼泪。
这也是海的形状。它的透明
涌自同一个更深的心灵。
即使把两袋水加一起，不影响
它的宽广。它们仍然很新鲜，
仿佛就会游出两尾鲱鱼。
你用它浇细沙似的面粉，
锻炼的面包，也是海的形状。
还未用利帆切开时，
已像一艘远去的轮船。
桌上剩下的这对塑料袋，
也是海的形状。在变扁，
像潮水慢慢退下了沙滩。
真正的潮水退下沙滩时，
献上的盐，也是海的形状。
你不信？我应该拎回一袋水，

Jiang Hao

Jiang Hao, born in Chongqing in 1971, has been an editor, a journalist, a book designer, and a substitute teacher in Chengdu, Beijing, Hainan, and Ürümqi. He was the founder of the magazine *New Poetry* and has been its chief editor since 2002. He has published collections of both poetry and essays.

Translated by Thomas Moran

THE SHAPE OF THE SEA

Every time you ask me about the shape of the sea,
I should go get two bags of seawater.
This is the shape of the sea, it's like a pair of eyes;
Or rather this is the shape of the sea as seen by eyes.
Touch it, it's like wiping away
Two hot teardrops.
This is also the shape of the sea. Its transparency
Rises up from the same depth of heart.
You can put the bags together but it won't change
The sea's dimension. The water stays clean and clear,
As if at any moment two herring might swim up.
You can sprinkle it on flour as fine as sand,
And toughen it into bread, the sea takes that shape, too.
Even before you slice it open with a sharp sail,
It looks like a steamer off in the distance.
These two plastic bags left on the table,
The sea takes their shape, too. They are flattening out,
Like a beach after the tide has slowly ebbed.
Salt laid in offering on a beach by a real tide
Is also the shape of the sea.
You don't believe me? I should go get one bag of water

一袋沙。这也是海的形状。
你肯定，否定；又不肯定，
不否定？你自己反复实验吧。
这也是你的形状。但你说，
"我只是我的形象。"

2003，10，30，海甸岛

游仙诗

1

涂抹有限纱窗，勾勒出沙漠的胸肌。
灯，递至下唇，融化。静电如发，
束之高岗。坐化的唱片，倒回到
两股的鹊桥，斜拉钢绳，悬起半壁
江山；冰淇淋峰顶，修饰你的双鬓。

我呢？衣袋里折叠的月亮，拧紧的
树冠，多少松弛的皮影，被演奏！
一车站激情，炫耀于踮起的浪尖；
你临风斜踏，大海蹩躞到阑珊一边。
但曲径深喉，牵连进胸襟，从这里，

捻出花絮中青丝的镊子，在纸包的
微火中，越轨锻炼。我承受想象，
部分卷入现实的非分；你的天真，
驭痉挛的云雨：自然，相克，相生。

And one bag of sand. This, too, is the shape of the sea.
You affirm it, you deny it; but then you don't affirm it,
And don't deny it? Try it yourself a few times.
This is also your shape. But you say,
"I'm just an image of myself."

30 October 2003, Haidian Island

A POEM OF A WANDERING IMMORTAL

1

A smear on the limited window screen sketches the contours of the
     desert's pectorals.
Lamplight passes the lower lip and dissolves. Static electricity fuzzes up
     like hair
Piled on the high hills. The record album has spun to its passing and
     returns
To the two-sectioned Magpie Bridge whose angled steel cables lift up
Half the land; ice-cream peaks decorate your temples.

Me? Pockets full of folded moonlight and tree crowns
Twisted down tight, so many slack shadow puppets perform!
All the emotions of the station are paraded on crests of waves on tiptoe;
You approach, leaning into the wind, and the ocean sidles off to the side.
But down the throat to the heart and then out from there

Tweezers that pick strands of silky black hair from amid the miscellany
Are tempered to transgression in small fires held in paper. I accept
     imagination,
And a portion of impropriety folded into reality; your naiveté,
Rides on spasms of clouds and rain: natural, mutually restricting,
     mutually enhancing.

2

天然呢？亲而密，肩胛涌出一排树：
喜悦，说不出孤单，必须的伶牙、
俐齿，三年有半，我咀嚼地平线，
积雪问心；可这里也一样冷，脆弱。
你读过的书，留住文字局？但现实

炙手可热：一念三千，随喜换美元。
爱欲诱惑出文明，学生头梳诗的
抑扬格；那时，教育误导的浪漫，
长相守不如长相知？私心谁不向往：
白马非马。你携烟酒，猛灌楼梯口；

夜如何其？着火的星相，爱的戏剧。
我说，我们去泰山，看太阳出入，
安慰贫穷天空？载回山水来文身，
请熟悉我的陌生美：勿巧笑扮祈祷。

2006，4，10，乌鲁木齐

2

Is it all natural? Up close and personal, shoulder blades heave up a line
of trees:
With delight, loneliness beyond words, requisite glibness
And a ready tongue, I have chewed over this horizon for three years and
a half.
A snowpack of introspection; but this place is just as cold, just as frail.
Those books you've read, will you leave them in the repository? But the
power of the real world

Is mighty: all existence is present in a single thought, you can
exchange it for dollars at your bliss.
Longing for love had seduced civilization into being, students comb
poems in iambic pentameter
From their hair; at the time, romanticism was misled by education.
Is lasting togetherness not as good as lasting understanding? Who
doesn't want to be selfish?
A white horse is not a horse. With cigarettes and wine you flooded the
stairway landing;

How goes the night? A horoscope caught on fire, a theater of love.
I ask, shall we go to Mt. Tai and watch the sun come and go,
And console our impoverished sky? We can bring back the landscape to
tattoo ourselves.
Please get to know my unfamiliar beauty: and no artful smiles as you
pretend to pray.

10 April 2006, Ürümqi

Jiang Hao   245

过白茫雪山

1

蓝月亮峡谷：名字的虚构来自一次更早的虚构。
还未苏醒的金沙江搂着四分之一个月亮
被期望漂得翠蓝的月亮，停留在残缺的月亮。
回到山脚的寺院日趋圆满，
一百二十名喇嘛充实着轮回的逆流，和八百个经桶一起
在原地旋转，既不深入，也不离开。

2

上山。崭新的客车就是新出炉的面包
没入刺眼的奶油，突如其来的白。
三只灰雕收拢着翅膀，在树木的残骸中站立
用警觉的眼神让雪吹得更远。
在某个时刻，我期待一个可以呼唤的名字
和我一起被飞雪擦亮。

Ma Hua

Ma Hua, born in Tianjin in 1972, received a degree in international politics from Fudan University, where he began writing poems and plays and served as head of the Yanyuan Drama Society. In 2004 the Jeep in which he was a passenger was lost in the Lancang River; his body was never recovered.

Translated by Paul Manfredi

CROSSING BAIMANG SNOW MOUNTAIN

1

Blue moon valley: the name's fabrication comes of a previous
    fabrication.
The still-unconscious Jinsha River embraces a quarter moon,
A moon washed green-blue by expectation, a moon staid in brokenness.
The temple in the foothills is fuller day by day,
120 lamas fill out the countercurrent of transmigrating souls, with
    800 sutra
Wheels spinning in place, neither deepening nor departing.

2

Up the mountain. Brand-new passenger car is a bun fresh out of
    the oven
Plunging into eye-piercing buttery whiteness; all at once
Three gray vultures draw in their wings, perched on the remains of tree
    branches
With vigilant gaze causing the snow to blow farther.
At some point, I await a name that can be called
Will be wiped clean in the blowing snow.

3

垭口的海拔众说纷纭，一块石碑
制止了所有人的争辩：4320米。
寒冷抽干生机
落石碾碎睡意。
风吹雪飞，隔年的积雪被一起翻出来，
几乎和今年的一样白。

4

对雪的疲乏使另一尊雪山的出现变得平淡。
困顿和暮色一起笼罩
被江水纠缠的山路。
突然到来的尽头正如期待的那样：
县城在山坳里浮起，雪山和流水在身后隐去
和白昼一起消失在想象中的远方。

3

The elevation at the pass is a matter of contention, but a stone tablet
Ends the debate: 4,320 meters.
Cold saps vitality,
Falling stones shatter sleepiness.
Wind blows, snow flies and with it the snow of years gone by
Looking as white as this year's.

4

The appearance of a new snow mountain is muted by weariness
        with snow.
Exhaustion and twilight envelop
A mountain road entangled in rivers.
The sudden arrival of the end satisfies all expectations:
A small town floating up in the mountain's cavern, the snow mountain
        and rushing
Waters recede behind us and with daylight disappear into remoteness
        of imagination.

沐浴在本城

献给异乡人的家乡

细小的雪在暗处推动我。入口处的陌生男人
替代我走进浴室，他呼出的酒气，像鱼儿钻进大海
汇入扑面而来的，更多浴客呵出的积雨云。他甚至
坠入了行走的梦中，翘起拇指，夸赞多年不见
而仍能一饮而尽的谢黑桃。河水的温度
让他醒了一会儿，他以为梦见了火山
却发现只不过是冲浪池吞没了
自己。他坚持睁着眼走进桑拿房，舀起一瓢水
泼向木箱中的火山岩。尖声跳起的水汽
带给他难得的伤感——家乡占有了他的每一个假期
就像婚姻买断了忠贞的女人，直到她不再年轻。

Han Bo

Han Bo was born in 1973 in Heilongjiang Province's city of Mudanjiang. Between 1991 and 1999, he was a student in the Department of International Politics and the School of Journalism at Fudan University, where he received a bachelor's degree in law and a master's degree in literature. In 1990 he founded the Night Walk Drama Studio and wrote and directed several plays. He has published two collections of poetry.

Translated by Jonathan S. Noble

BATHING IN THIS TOWN

dedicated to the hometown of a stranger

Fine snow propels me within darkness. At the entrance, a stranger,
    a man,
Replaces me and walks into a bathhouse. He exhales alcohol, like a fish
    darting into the ocean
And merging into the rain clouds puffed out by many bath patrons.
    He even
Falls into a dream of ambling about, giving a thumbs-up, praising the
    long-lost
Xie Heitao for being able to knock back the shots. The river's temperature
Wakes him up for a while—he thought he had dreamed of a volcano,
But rather discovered that a wave pool had engulfed
Him. Fighting to keep his eyes open, he walks into the sauna, scoops a
    ladle of water,
Splashes it on the wooden box's volcanic rocks. Steam jumps up, shrilly,
Triggering in him an unusual melancholy—each vacation is occupied
    by his hometown
Just like a woman whose chastity is bought out by marriage until the
    day her youth is gone forever.

他把湿毛巾蒙在脸上，绝不是因为羞愧，他觉得
自己早已过了那个年龄，他只是为了躲避热浪
能够呼吸，能够不去看身边那群搓泥的河马。
酒精被汗水一点一点挤出身体，他离开
堆满便便大腹的木凳，走向冰水池
但只伸进去一个手指，就打消了念头
他强调自己是温带的生物，应该在适宜的
水温里，完成进茶前的沐浴。

细小的雪覆盖了我和脚下农民承包的田埂。他们的女儿
呆在二楼，他的对面，休息室入口的沙发上
这里是她们耕作的田埂。他的出现
让她们失望，他的脸上写着报纸上描述的未来
那是一桩乏味透顶的事，不允许任何一个男人专有的
女人，将被任何一个男人专有。相比之下
她们更欣赏跑来跑去，一心想为女客捏脚的茶童
那孩子嘴上刚冒出一层绒毛，却装着一肚子
谜语、笑料和段子，如果缺了他，这个世界
将是倒立的，就像一种挺艺术的姿势。她
离开顾镜自怜的她们，走向正在抠脚、喝茶的他
他不是一匹河马，但她坚信自己海豹般的姿势
能够让他搁浅，她的手指，弹奏了几下空气，又轻轻
划过他的锦囊，她要向他推销四十分钟
神圣的黑暗，帮助他，回到母亲为他缔造的黑暗中
让想象力为他施洗。他个是教徒，所能做的

He covers his face with a damp towel, not at all out of shame but
    because he feels
He has already passed that age, and he wants to avoid the waves of heat
So he can breathe, and he doesn't have to see those mud-rubbing
    hippos next to him.
The alcohol is squeezed out of his body, drop by drop, through sweat,
    and he leaves
The wooden bench stacked with potbellies, and walks toward the ice-
    water pool,
But one touch of a finger and he changes his mind.
He stresses he is a temperate zone life form and should
Bathe in water heated to a suitable temperature before he can enjoy
    his tea.

Fine snow covers me and the farmers' land under my feet. Their
    daughters
Stay on the second floor. Across from him, there's a sofa at the lounge's
    entrance:
These are the fields cultivated by the women. His appearance
Disappoints them. The future, as described by a newspaper, is written
    on his face—
That's a totally drab thing, women who won't allow any man to possess
Them but will be possessed by any man. In contrast
The women prefer the tea boy, running to and fro, devoted to
    massaging the feet of female customers.
Fuzz sprouts from above the boy's lip, but he has a belly full of
Riddles, jokes, and dirty stories—without him, the world
Would be upside down, like a supremely artistic pose. She
Leaves the self-pitying women, and walks toward the tea-drinking,
    foot-picking him.
He is not a hippo, but she's confident her seal-like posture
Can beach him; her fingers, strumming the air, gently
Brushing against his billfold, she wants to sell him forty minutes of
Sacred darkness, helping him return to the darkness created by his
    mother,
To be baptized by his imagination. He's not a believer, all he can do

只是胡乱夸奖，他搬出她所信服的人生巅峰的
化身：电影明星、歌星、模特、青春大使、形象代言人
而他自己只是个火车司机，明天就要下岗，就要跌入
人生的谷底。他为她们的牺牲而感慨，但无力购买
这半个人类的节日。她听到了她们吃吃的笑声，在背后
就像一堆爬上她脊背的蛇，而她的脚下踩着松软的
田埂，她和向日葵们站在一起，那是她父亲
亲手种下的，她的门齿上，还留着它们果实的痕迹。

细小的雪从内部挤压我。新续的菊花
在我黑暗的管道中流淌。写诗的时候，我
梦见了什么，一种魔法？一种叙述不是来自
主动者，而是来自被动者，它就孕育着避雷针的
魔力？我洗浴着，我蒸发着，我阴干着
我提着壶，我运着力，我掀开镜子，我取出帽子
我忍受着怪味、汗水、疲惫、厌倦，我点上
一枝烟，然后又掐灭，我失足跌进水池。
叙述与替代使我苏醒，我扳动了
流水的轴，它就在那里，它改变着冲刷的速度
它衡量着快乐的密度，它为肉体的田野作证
它是兰汤，它是时光，它就是容纳我衰老的浑浊。

结绳宴会

我不爱吃绳子
我说，我不爱吃

Is spout praise, raising the pinnacles of success that she worships, the
Incarnates: movie stars, pop idols, supermodels, ambassadors of
         youth, endorsement celebrities—
But he is just a train conductor, who tomorrow will lose his job, falling
         into
Life's abyss. He feels sorry for the girl's sacrifices, but he has no money
         to buy
This holiday for half of humanity. She hears their giggles, behind her,
As if a bunch of snakes were climbing up her spine, but her feet tread
         upon the soft
Land. She and the sunflowers stand together—that her father,
Planted by his own hands, her incisors still contain their fleshy bits.

Fine snow squeezes me from inside. The new batch of chrysanthemums
Flow within my dark tunnel. When writing poetry, I
Dream of what, a type of magic? Narration doesn't come from
A creator, but rather comes from the receiver, it contains a lightning
         rod of
Magical powers? I bathe, I steam, I lie out to dry,
I carry a pot, I use force, I turn over a mirror, I remove a hat,
I tolerate the strange odor, the sweat, the exhaustion, the weariness,
         I light
A cigarette and then put it out. I slip and fall into the pool.
Narrative and displacement awaken me. I turn on
The tap for water, there it is, it changes the speed of the water's flow,
It measures the density of happiness, it corroborates the fields of flesh.
It is bathwater, it is time, it is the murkiness that embraces my
         getting old.

KNOT-TYING BANQUET

I don't like eating rope
I say, I don't like eating it

那是盘子吗
那都是绳子，嘴里叼着尾巴

真是抱歉，他勒紧领带
盘子破了，晚餐只剩一个轮廓

但是，难道你不想尝尝秘密
他的手指插进绳圈，轻轻搅动空气

把舌头伸进圈套，就这样
没有人知道你在品尝

我伸出筷子
绳圈里有旋涡，有一张我看不见的嘴

她在用力
她在勒紧筷子的脖子

她想跟你交谈，他说
她饿，她以为你要喂给她隐私

他细心地舔着手指
眼角瞄着筷子，它们已经窒息

你，写过小说吗？知不知道
如何编织一个不露破绽的故事

她，是位出色的小说家
我的这根手指，就是她虚构的

她的脑袋，一度套进自己编织的故事
脖子上打着死结，就像这双筷子

我喂给她我的秘密：我
是一根身怀杂技的绳子

Is that a plate?
It's all rope, a tail hanging out of a mouth

I'm really sorry, he tightens his tie
The plate broke, only an outline remains from dinner

But, don't you want to taste the secret?
His finger is inserted into a lasso, gently stirring the air

Stick your tongue into a trap, just like this
No one will know you are tasting it

I hold out chopsticks
There's an eddy in the lasso, a mouth invisible to me

She uses great effort
She is tightening the neck of the chopsticks

She wants to speak with you, he says
She's hungry, she thought you would feed her a secret

He carefully licks a finger
Glancing at the chopsticks out of a corner of his eye, they have already
        suffocated

You, have you written a novel? Do you know
How to weave a story without giving it away?

She is an outstanding novelist
This finger of mine, is fabricated by her

Her head, once looped into her own story
A fast knot tied on the neck, like this pair of chopsticks

I feed her my secret: I
Am a rope with acrobatic skill

如果她本是一张瓷盘，我
就可以直立，让她在我的头顶旋转

我没想到，她也是一根绳子
首尾相衔，远看就像一张瓷盘

她说，来吧，这又不是第一次
让我给你织一双手套

可是，她是，第一次
她第一次打成一个活结

在她的编织中，我进进出出
她需要故事，我需要她

她问：一条蛇需要吊死另一条蛇
我答：生活都是虚构的囚徒

我问：结绳的游戏需要织进多少观众
她答：虚构，饥饿的赴宴者

我，不想吃绳子
我说，我还是不想吃绳子

他举起手指，模仿一根绳子的直立
然后又突然将它藏进手心，爆出一个指响

这是什么意思？我说
如果只有绳子，我这就回去

没什么意思，他摊开手心
我和她，在同一个结里编着各自的梦

真的没什么意思，我只是听说
饥饿的人，都是脱了结的绳子

If she were a porcelain plate, I
Could stand erect, letting her spin on my head

I never thought, she is also a rope
Linked end to end, from afar looks like a porcelain plate

She says, come, this is not the first time
Let me knit a pair of gloves for you

But, for her, it is the first time
The first time she tied a slipknot

In her knitting, I come in and out
She needs stories, I need her

She asks: does a snake need to hang another snake to death?
I answer: life is but a prisoner of fiction

I ask: how many readers does the knot-tying game need to weave in?
I answer: fiction, starving banqueters

I don't want to eat rope
I say, I still don't want to eat rope

He raises a finger, sticking up so as to imitate a rope
Then suddenly hides it in the palm, blasting out a finger's snap

What does that mean? I say
If only rope, then I will go back

No meaning, he spreads open the palm
She and I, we weave our separate dreams in the same knot

Really no meaning, I just heard
Hungry people, all are ropes that have been untied.

梳形桥

风从对立的两极
缓缓吹来
马克·斯特兰德

积郁已久的鼻孔和柿树和长椅
这是一场简朴的婚礼
一个驼背的女孩担任临时的侍者
匆匆走着
顶着一只洗净发亮的杯子

醉汉在墙根低声呕吐
低声弄湿了黑色的礼服

他发现墙上有一道豁口在张开
有一个黑影在墙外
背着身
拴马
他感到带有肉翅的幼鼠
正踩着他的头跳舞——
那人会从这豁口跳过来！

雨水腾出一间空空的屋子
而那人只住短短一夜

Leng Shuang

Leng Shuang was born in 1973. After graduating from high school in 1990, he went on to study in the Chinese department of Peking University. He has worked as a journalist and is currently a lecturer at the Minzu University of China. His first poetry collection was published in 2008.

Translated by Heather Inwood

COMB-SHAPED BRIDGE

The wind comes from opposite poles,
traveling slowly.
MARK STRAND

Long-stifled nostrils, persimmon trees and benches
this is a simple wedding
a hunchbacked girl's a makeshift waitress
walking hurriedly
her head carrying a sparkling clean glass

a drunk quietly vomits by the foot of the wall
quietly soiling his black suit

through a crack in the wall he spies
a black shadow on the other side
back turned
tethering a horse
he feels a young rat with fleshy wings
dancing on top of his head—
that person will jump through the crack!

The room is empty, vacated by the rain
yet that person will stay just one short night

我们年龄的雾

它是怎么来的：这是一个谜。
并非无法解开，只是我宁愿
为自己保留少许神秘性。

如同一只蜗牛，顺着台阶，
贴着墙，我目力所及之处
都已留下它牛乳般的痕迹：

我有意忽略了它的重量，
不过，这倒是因为我深知
它的力量。我已领略过多次。

同样，我也从不担心
能见度之类的问题：我注意到
在它腹中有一所漂浮的邮局。

就这样，一日三餐，夜间散步，
睡前读几页帕斯卡尔。
窗户开着。我感到了变化。

因此我一度最感兴趣的是
它的边缘究竟在哪里，
结果总是使我暗自惊叹。

而现在我已有信心把它装进
口袋，像一盒火柴，可以照明，
可以取暖，可以做算命游戏。

并且我允许它变作一只蚂蚁
溜出来，看着它从我的手臂
钻进我的胸腔，我承认，痒——

THE FOG OF OUR AGE

How it got here is a puzzle.
That's not to say it's unsolvable, but I'd rather
keep a little mystery for myself.

Snail-like, up the steps,
against the wall; wherever I look
I see its milky trail:

I intentionally ignore its weight,
but this is because I know
its strength. I've sensed it many times.

Similarly, I never worry about
questions of visibility and the like: I've noticed
a post office floating in its belly.

Just like that, three meals a day, take strolls at night,
read a few pages of Pascal before bed.
The window's open. I've felt the change.

Because of this, I was for a time most engrossed
with where its edges lie—
this always left me full of secret wonder.

But now I have the confidence to stuff it
in a pocket like a box of matches, good for a light,
good for warmth, or for a fortune-telling game.

I also let it turn into an ant and
slip out, watch it cross my arm,
burrow into my chest where, I admit, it tickles—

你掀开我灵魂九曲连环的入口，
而这正像我始终好奇的那样：当我
看见你时，我已在你之中

You have opened the labyrinthine entrance to my soul,
and as curious as I've always been: when I see you
I am already within you.

聚集

冬雨聚集起全部的泪
湿漉漉的落叶犹如黑色的纸钱

一个男人在上坡，他竖起的肩膀
聚集起全部的隐忍

松针间的鸟，聚集起全部的灰
雨丝如飘发，聚集成一张美丽的脸

我站在窗前，看那玻璃上的水滴
聚集成悲伤的海

什么样的悲伤会聚集成力
取决于你的爱

Duo Yu

Duo Yu, born in 1973 in Shandong, is a scholar and writer. In 1994 he graduated from the Chinese department of Beijing Normal University. In 2000 he joined friends in starting the Lower Body poetry movement. He has received several independent poetry prizes and has published collections of poetry and essays on literary history. He now lives in Tianjin where, in addition to writing poetry and essays, he edits the independent poetry journal *Poem Time*.

Translated by Steve Riep

GATHERING UP

The winter rain gathers up all the tears
dampening fallen leaves black, like burnt spirit money,

A man trudging uphill, his raised shoulders
gather up all forbearance,

The bird in the pine needles gathers up all the ash gray
threads of rain, like hair floating in the wind, gather up into a
      beautiful face,

I stand by the window, looking at the water droplets on the pane
gathering up to form a sea of sorrow,

What sort of sorrow will, when gathered up, become a force
depends on your love.

乡村史

德宗三年，英军行于沪宁道上
湘乡薨，举人们忙于作挽联
王二忙于在小亚麻布衫里捉虱子……

……那秋日的雨，一直下到今天
一拨又一拨的愁云，仿佛秋天的心
风物冰凉，小流氓也感到无聊
庄稼慵懒地长着，麦子躺在瓮里
张家的门紧闭，李家的狗
学会了沉思
一些人在廊下支起桌子，打牌
其中就有我死去多年的爷爷
闲暇贴在睫毛上，鞋子逸出了脚面
有人打太极摇扇子
有人读论语说废话
有人登高有人纳妾有人偷欢
偷到了心烦。还没到时间
还没到结党营社读水浒的时间
还没到磨刀自渎写密信的时间
还没到张灯佩剑孤独自饮的时间
还没到时间，雨水泡在雨水中
村长泡在寡妇家
粮食还在，灯绳还在，裤脚上的泥泞还在
民国远去了，还没到
重写的时间

VILLAGE HISTORY

In 1878, the third year of the Dezong Reign, English troops marched
      along the Shanghai-Nanjing Road,
At the death of Zeng Guofan, the provincial exam graduates busied
      themselves composing elegiac couplets,
Wang Second busied himself catching the lice in his short linen shirt...

...The rain on that autumn day has fallen steadily down to today
wave after wave of gloomy clouds, like the heart of autumn
ice-cold scenery, which would bore even the least of hooligans,
the crops grow languidly, wheat lies in earthen vats,
the Zhang family's door is shut tight, the Li family's dog
learned how to ponder,
some people set up tables under the verandas, and play cards
—among them my long-dead granddad—
leisure rests on the eyelashes, shoes removed from feet;
some do tai chi exercises while fanning themselves,
some read *The Analects* and talk nonsense,
while some climb mountains, some take concubines, and some dally,
dally until they are bored. And it is not yet time,
not yet time to form a clique to read the *Water Margin,*
not yet time to sharpen a knife, abuse oneself, or write secret letters,
not yet time to hang up lanterns, wear a sword at one's waist, or
      drink alone,
not yet time; rainwater steeping in rainwater
the village head dallies at the widow's home
the grain is still there, the lantern wicks are still there, the mud on the
      trouser leg is still there,
the Republic has long since gone, not yet time
for rewriting.

一个拣鲨鱼牙齿的男人

给臧棣

一个拣鲨鱼牙齿的男人，
弓着腰、撅着已近中年的屁股，
在沙与海水之间搜寻。
换做在他的故乡、他的童年，
这个姿势更像是在把少年水稻
插进东亚泥土旺盛的生殖循环里。
但请相信我，此刻他的确是在
拣鲨鱼的牙齿，在佛罗里达的
萨拉索塔县，在一个
叫做玛纳索塔的狭长的小岛西侧
濒临墨西哥湾的海滩上。
像着了魔一般，他已经拣了
整整一个下午，虽然灼人的烈日
似要将他熔成一团白光，但
每拣得一颗牙齿，他就感觉身上
多了一条鲨鱼的元气。那些

Hu Xudong

Hu Xudong (Continuing Winter), pen name of Hu Xudong (Sunrising East), was born in Chongqing in 1974. He received his PhD from Peking University and is an associate professor at the Graduate Institute of World Literature, Peking University. He has published volumes of poetry and collections of essays. He has taught at the Universidade de Brasília and participated in the International Writing Program at the University of Iowa by invitation of the State Department.

Translated by Kuo-ch'ing Tu
(with assistance from Robert Backus)

A MAN WHO COLLECTS SHARK TEETH
for Zang Di

A man who collects shark teeth,
arches his body and sticks up his near-midlife hips,
searching between the sand and the water.
If it were his hometown, and childhood,
this posture would look more like thrusting young rice seedlings
into the East Asian soil's vigorous reproductive cycle.
But trust me, at the moment he is actually
collecting shark teeth in Florida,
in Sarasota County on the west side
of a long narrow island called Manasota Key,
off a beach in the Gulf of Mexico.
He has been collecting them as if possessed
the entire afternoon, although the burning sun
seems ready to fuse him into a sphere of white light.
But whenever he picks up a tooth, he feels
energized with the vigor of one more shark. Those teeth,

乌黑、闪亮、带着不容置疑的
撕咬的迫切性的牙齿，是被海水
挽留下来的力量的颗粒，是
静止在细沙里的嗜血的加速度，
是大海深处巨大的残暴之美被潮汐
颠倒了过来，变成了小小一枚
美之残暴。他紧攥着这些
余威尚存的尖利的小东西，这些
没有皮肉的鲨鱼，想象着
在深海一样昏暗的中年生活里，
自己偶尔也能朝着迎面撞来的厄运
亮出成千上万颗鲨鱼的牙齿。

2008，11，20，Manasota Key，Florida

一个在海滩上朗诵的男人

一个在海滩上朗诵的男人
从来都没有想到他会像现在这样
盘腿坐在沙滩上，跟海浪
比赛大嗓门。他的听众，一群
追逐夕阳定居在佛罗里达西海岸的
退休老人，从各自的家中带来了
沙滩折叠椅，笑眯眯地，
听他沙哑的嗓音如何在半空中一种
叫做诗的透明的容器里翻扬，而后
落在地上，变成他们脚下
细小的沙砾。只有他自己注意到：
每首诗，当他用汉语朗诵的时候，
成群的海鸟会在他头顶上
用友善的翅膀标示出每个字的
声调；而当他用笨拙的英语
朗诵译本的时候，不是他，
而是一个蹩脚的演员，躲在

jet-black, flashing with an unquestionably
urgent biting desire, are nuggets of force
kept behind by the ocean water,
bloodthirsty acceleration set quiet in the sand,
beauties of an enormous cruelty hidden in the depths of the ocean,
rolled up by the tide and transfigured
into piecemeal cruelties of a single beauty. He firmly grasps
these still-powerful sharp pointed tiny objects, these
skinless fleshless sharks, and imagines himself
in a midlife dark like the ocean depths,
by chance able to flash thousands of shark teeth
against an oncoming collision with disaster.

20 November 2008, Manasota Key, Florida

A MAN RECITING ALOUD ON THE BEACH

A man reciting aloud on the beach
never thought he would be doing this,
sitting crossed-legged on the beach in competition with the waves
to see who has the louder voice. His audience, a group of retirees
who have chased the sunset and settled on the west coast of Florida,
have brought folding beach chairs from their homes,
and break into smiles as they listen to
his gravelly voice spiral airborne in the
transparent receptacle called poetry,
and then fall to the ground to become
fine grit under their feet. Only he is aware:
whenever he recites a poem in Chinese,
a flock of seagulls will use friendly wings over his head
to indicate each character's tone;
and when he uses his clumsy English
to recite the text in translation, it is not he who speaks
but a halting thespian who hides behind his Adam's apple

他的喉结里，练习一个外国配角
古怪的台词。朗诵中，他抬头
望向远方，天尽头，贤惠的大海
正在唤回劳作了一整天的太阳。
一瞬间，他觉得自己也成了
听众的一员，一个名字叫风的
伟大的诗人，不知何时凑近了
别在他衣领上的麦克风，在他
稍事停顿之时，风开始用
从每一扇贝壳、每一片树叶上
借来的声音，朗诵最不朽的诗句：
沉默，每小时17英里的沉默。

2008，11，23，Manasota Key，Florida

and rehearses the outlandish lines
of a foreign actor in a supporting role. As he recites
he raises his head and gazes off into the distance, there
where the sky ends, and Goodwife Sea
is calling Sun to come home after a full day's labor.
In that instant the man feels that he too has become
a member of the audience, and before he knows it
a great poet by the name of Wind closes in
on the microphone clipped to his collar; and when
for a moment he pauses, Wind begins to use the sound
it borrows from every shell and leaf
to recite the one imperishable poetic line:
silence, a silence at seventeen miles per hour.

23 November 2008, Manasota Key, Florida

送别诗

草木已腓，柳枝毪毪，
古戍道劝风停的亭子，
劝酒的天涯，悲之杯。
雁叫是满心耳的轻雷，
画角王孙带电的徂年。
我送你这诗中的热冰。

所谓宇宙不过是
你是南而我是北，
你是平而我是仄。

巴丹吉林

老路陷溺，新路易被吹散，
吉普醉汉，那就试试无路，
时而低飞。
快失重的我们拥挤、坠泻，
斜冲上浪峰，像一首艳诗。

这一幕熟稔，童年像死后
玩着沙子；迷宫几乎流水。

Qin Xiaoyu

Qin Xiaoyu was born in 1974 in Hohhot, Inner Mongolia. He has published a collection of poems and edited an anthology of poetry.

FAREWELL: A POEM

translated by Howard Y.F. Choy

Wilted grass and trees, wispy willow twigs,
Ancient frontier station trying to stay the wind,
Bottoms up! At the ends of the earth, my melancholy cup.
Wild geese cry a distant thunder in my heart's ears,
Painted bugles, princely nobles, electrically fleeting years.
This poem is a gift of hot ice for you.

What we call the universe merely means
You are south, I am north.
You are level tone, I am oblique.

BADANJILIN DESERT

translated by Shelley Wing Chan

The old road has sunk, the new one is easily blown away,
Jeep, my drunkard, let's try driving without a road,
flying low once in a while.
Weightlessly, we are crammed together and rushing down,
obliquely surfing the crests of waves, like an erotic poem.

This act I know so well, childhood is like after death
playing with sand; water almost flows in the labyrinth.

你是沙做的沙漏，
漏下的沙子，组成了沙漠。
诗之蚌磨砺不肯漏下的沙。

海子浊黄，缘于它的清澈，
它多像个诱你幽媾的女鬼，
对于巴丹吉林，它的
曲线认同而它的平旷反对。
你多想做它野鸭飞起的岸，

摸遍它的梦境，舔它的涩，
久久地听它无声处的驼铃。
天地玄黄的凝视。你跻身
自恋的芦苇，徘徊又临照，
像艳诗，空被满溢地盛着。

包钢尾矿坝

尾矿坝巍峨，矿湖高悬。
堤头，小蛇似的几茎草。
坝内刺鼻的热湖，
浓白的矿浆多么激烈。

它氤氲，
不同于包钢储煤厂的泼墨。
钎入土，
化疗的沥青与泡沫的深井；铀走的黄河。

You are an hourglass made of sand,
the sand that slides down forms a desert.
The sand rhyme-clam hardens the sand not willing to slide down.

The muddy yellow lake originates from its limpidity,
how it looks like a phantom seductress luring you into sex,
with Badanjilin; its
curve approves but its levelness opposes.
You so want to be its shore from which wild ducks fly,

to fondle its dream, to lick its bitterness,
to linger while listening to its camel bells in silence.
The gaze of heaven and earth. You place yourself
among the narcissistic reeds, wandering and mirroring,
like an erotic poem, with emptiness yet filled to bursting.

TAILING DAM OF BAOTOU STEEL

translated by Shelley Wing Chan

Tailing dam stands tall, mine lake hangs high.
At dike's end stand a few grasses, snakelike.
In the dam, the hot lake assails the nostrils;
dense and white, the molten ore is so fierce.

It is in the mist,
not the splashed ink of Baotou Steel's coal yard.
Thorium gets into the soil,
the chemo pitch and deep, foamy well; in the Yellow River uranium
    whirls.

新长征路上的摇滚

13岁那天我阴着手
在机耕路上
游荡。
大风，大太阳
水田漫天荒芜。
右脚前方五六步远，
一只鸟
蹦了出去，
划破我的眼眶。
"到夏天你也许就是大人啦。"
这个大年初一的清晨，妈说
阿姐出场还要早。

在被窝里我没动，手心有点湿
有点慌。

半分钟后，滚滚红尘卷着
一骑摩托上的男女
刮跑脚边
我薄冰似的影子。
她一手搂抱他腰，
一手拎了录音机轰响
他们疾飞。

Shen Mujin

Shen Mujin was born in 1975 in Zhejiang Province and lives in Beijing. She is a freelance photographer as well as a poet and has self-published two poetry collections.

Translated by Heather Inwood

ROCK AND ROLL ON THE NEW LONG MARCH

The day I turned thirteen
I loitered with chilly hands
along a tractor path.
The wind was strong, the sun was bright,
paddy fields filled the barren skies.
Five or six paces ahead of my right foot,
a bird
shot out,
lacerating my eyes.
"Maybe by summertime you'll be a grown-up!"
On this New Year's dawn Ma said
Big Sis will be out even sooner.

Under the covers I didn't move an inch, my palms were a little damp,
a little flurried.

Half a minute later, balls of red dust kicked up
by a motorcycling couple
blew away my ice-thin shadow
beside my feet.
With her one hand hugging his waist,
the other holding a boom box,
they flew like the wind.

他们看上去危险
又诱人。

仿佛云端
砸下一声吼——
"一二三四五六、呀
七"

2005，12，18

妮可 • 基德曼在蒸汽时代

蒸汽时代
像大鸟
伸着笨拙、滚烫的脖子，
赫吃　赫吃
哈着白雾。白日梦似雾。
生活沸腾
在车头上一团团
棉花糖里。

"……我是贵族。"
沦陷在屠宰场里，还是贵族；
妮可拔着鸡毛和鸭毛，
忽见他骑着一道刺亮的弧线
飞过海峡。
蒸汽时代阿汤哥
很有种，
为还未属于他的女人
去决斗，
存心去死。
蒸汽时代，妮可•基德曼当然
被骚气冲天的新生活喝斥。
"——他娘的
我发誓要挣得我的土地"

They looked dangerous
yet alluring.

It was as if the clouds had
smashed out a roar:
"one two three four five six yeah
seven"

18 December 2005

NICOLE KIDMAN IN THE AGE OF STEAM

In the age of steam
like a big bird
stretching its clumsy, boiling-hot neck,
huffing and puffing
white fog. Daydreams are like fog.
Above the carriage
inside balls of cotton candy
life bubbles.

"...I am nobility."
Fallen in the slaughterhouse, still nobility;
Nicole plucks chicken and duck feathers,
suddenly sees him riding a shining arc,
soaring across the ocean.
In the age of steam
Tom has balls,
fighting to the end for a woman
who's not yet his,
resolving to meet his death.
In the age of steam, Nicole Kidman is of course
railed at by her roguish new life.
"...goddamn it
I swear I'm gonna get my land!"

柔弱胸膛里忽的
升腾起

大地雄心。

2006，11，23

轻蔑

她趴在桌上，
像只不会说话的鸟。
垂落指尖，垂落毛。
失望是静电慢慢消失的过程。
失望是饮弹后把头偏向一隅
蔑视自己。

2007，2，6

Ambition swells suddenly from a weak chest

in a land far and away.

23 November 2006

DISDAIN

She is sprawled across the desk
like a bird that can't talk.
Drooping fingers, drooping feathers.
Disappointment is the slow disappearance of static electricity.
Disappointment is turning your head to one side after swallowing
      a bullet,
loathing yourself.

6 February 2007

我曾经爱过的螃蟹

第一次出海的时候
我仅仅有现在一半的身高
舅舅把一顶海军军帽扣在我的脑袋上
然后跳到水里，跟随鱼群
去了哥伦比亚，失去了他
和他的指引，我很快就自由了
海里的火焰比绸缎还要柔软
有些亮光，来自我在压力中旋转的心跳
有只螃蟹来与我攀谈，它告诉我一个事实
几千年来，全世界的螃蟹都在向陆地迁移，这个过程很慢
它们并不着急，它们随着潮汐跑上跑下，只是在前海
向前迈了很少的几步，它说它爱我，希望我们能够
分享这几个气泡，一起上岸，在秘密的岩石码头上
微笑着，我和几千只螃蟹握手，我希望和它们一样

Wang Ao

Wang Ao, born in the city of Qingdao in Shandong Province in 1976, has studied at Peking University, Washington University in St. Louis, and Yale, from which he received a PhD in literature in 2008. He is the author of several books of poetry, one of which won the Anne Kao Poetry Prize. He also translates literary criticism and contemporary Chinese and English poetry (including Stevens's *Harmonium*). He teaches in the US.

Translated by Daniel Bryant

THE CRAB I FELL IN LOVE WITH

When I first went to sea,
I was barely half as tall as I am now.
My uncle put a navy cap on my head,
Then jumped into the water and followed a school of fish
To Colombia; I lost him
And his guidance, and soon I was free.
The sea's flames were gentler than silk or satin.
Lights came from my heartbeat spinning under pressure.
A crab came to chat, it revealed something to me:
For thousands of years, the world's crabs have been moving toward the
        shore; this progress is quite slow,
They are in no rush. They run up and down with the tide, only in the
        foreshore.
It took a few steps forward, it said it loved me and hoped that we would
        be able
To share these bubbles. We went ashore together, on the secret
        stone jetty.
Smiling, I shook hands with a few thousand crabs, I hoped to be
        like them,

把骨头长在皮肤的外面，在脆弱的时刻，用太阳能补充盔甲中的钙
我们开始登山
　　　崂山的背面铺着一层墨绿
我们用手臂和钳子，震撼着它的花岗脉
当我赤裸地站在山顶，看到月亮正被一个黑影钳住
夜晚滴着水，它们沉默着，爬到我的身体上，让我轻轻地渗出血

2000

To grow a skeleton outside my skin, and when I was fragile, to
    replenish the calcium in my shell with sunlight.
We began to climb the mountain.
                      The back of Laoshan was covered with
    a layer of blackish green;
With our arms and claws, we shook its granite veins.
When I stood naked on the mountaintop, I saw that a black shape was
    clutching the moon.
The evening dripped water; they fell silent, crawled onto my body, so
    that I oozed a little blood.

2000

ABOUT THE EDITOR, TRANSLATION CO-EDITORS, AND TRANSLATORS

Editor QINGPING WANG was born in 1962. He studied at Peking University from 1983 to 1987 and majored in Chinese literature. He has been with the People's Literature Publishing House since 1987, moving to the position of editor for poetry and fiction in 2002. Mr. Wang has edited a long list of collections, including anthologies with works of Hai Zi, Shi Zhi, Xi Chuan, Wang Jiaxin, Xiao Kaiyu, and Sun Wenbo. As a poet, Mr. Wang was first published in 1982 in *Yuhua Magazine,* a journal produced in Nanjing. In 1996, he won the Liu Li-an Poetry Prize, at that time China's most prestigious award for a young poet.

Translation co-editor SYLVIA LI-CHUN LIN has translated many works by Chinese writers both on her own and in collaboration with Howard Goldblatt. Her latest book is *Representing Atrocity in Taiwan: The 2/28 Incident and White Terror in Fiction and Film.* As an associate professor of Chinese in the University of Notre Dame's Department of East Asian Languages and Cultures, Lin has researched modern and contemporary Chinese literature and culture and Chinese literature from Taiwan. Lin has been awarded the Translation of the Year Award, the Rev. Edmund P. Joyce, CSC, Award for Excellence in Undergraduate Teaching, and research grants from the University of Notre Dame and the Chiang Ching-kuo Foundation for International Scholarly Exchange. In 2009 she and Tze-lan D. Sang were awarded a grant by the American Council of Learned Societies (ACLS) to organize an international workshop on documentary films from Taiwan; they are currently co-editing the essays for publication.

Translation co-editor HOWARD GOLDBLATT has published English translations of fifty novels and story collections by writers from China, Taiwan, and Hong Kong. His translation (with Sylvia Li-chun Lin) of *Notes of a Desolate Man,* by the Taiwanese novelist Chu T'ien-wen, won the 1999 Translation of the Year Award given by the American Literary Translators Association. He has also authored or edited six books on Chinese literature. His most recent translations include Jiang Rong's *Wolf Totem,* winner of the 2007 Man Asian Literary Prize, Mo Yan's *Life and Death Are Wearing Me Out*, recipient of the 2009 Newman Prize for Chinese Literature, Su Tong's *Boat to Redemption*, winner of the 2009 Man Asian Literary Prize, and (again with Sylvia Li-chun Lin) Bi Feiyu's *Three Sisters*, recipient of the 2010 Man Asian Literary Prize. He has received two translation grants from the National Endowment for the Arts and, in 2009, a Guggenheim Fellowship.

TRANSLATORS

JOSEPH R. ALLEN is a professor of Chinese literature and former chair of Asian Languages and Literatures, University of Minnesota, Twin Cities. Trained in classical literature, Allen has edited, with additional translations, Arthur Waley's *The Book of Songs*. He has also written on contemporary Chinese poetry, including translation and commentary in *Forbidden Games & Video Poems: The Poetry of Yang Mu and Lo Ch'ing* and *Sea of Dreams: The Selected Works of Gu Cheng*. Allen came to Chinese poetry studies through an early encounter with Gary Snyder's *Riprap and Cold Mountain Poems*.

ROBERT BACKUS received his PhD in Oriental languages from the University of California, Berkeley, and spent most of his career at the University of California, Santa Barbara. He retired in 1991 and is currently serving as Professor Emeritus of Japanese Literature in the Department of East Asian Languages and Cultural Studies. His publications include a number of articles in the *Harvard Journal of Asiatic Studies* on Japanese Confucianism in the Edo period, the Kansei Reform and samurai education, and the work of the Edo-period Confucian Tsukada Taihō, together with a translation of his *Seidō tokumon* (Attaining the gates to the way of the sage). He wrote a book of literary translation, *The Riverside Counselor's Stories: Vernacular Fiction of Late Heian Japan*. Backus serves as co-editor of *Taiwan Literature: English Translation Series*, published at UCSB by the Forum for the Study of World Literatures in Chinese.

JOHN BALCOM is an award-winning translator of Chinese literature and a past president of the American Literary Translators Association. He lives in Monterey with his wife, Yingtsih, who is also a translator.

ALLAN H. BARR was born in Montreal, grew up in Britain, and now teaches Chinese at Pomona College in California. He has published extensively on *Liaozhai zhiyi*, the celebrated collection of strange tales by Pu Songling (1640–1715), and is currently writing a book on the Ming History Inquisition of 1663. In recent years he has translated several works by the contemporary Chinese author Yu Hua; his translation of Yu's debut novel, *Cries in the Drizzle*, was published in 2007.

DANIEL BRYANT is the author of *Lyric Poets of the Southern T'ang, Ho Ching-ming Ts'ung-k'ao, The Great Recreation: Ho Ching-ming (1483–1520) and His World*, and numerous articles, conference papers, reviews, and translations. Since his retirement from the University of Victoria, he has devoted himself to birding, recovering from a home reno, and averting his eyes from a shapeless monster housed in a document folder named "Book5."

CINDY M. CARTER is a Beijing-based translator of Chinese film, fiction, and poetry, and one of the founders of the Paper Republic website. Over the last decade, she has translated over forty documentary and feature films by indie directors, including Wang Bing, Zhao Liang, Huang Wenhai, and Wang Xiaoshuai. Her most recent fiction translation is of Yan Lianke's *Dream of Ding Village*. She is currently in-house translator and editor at the Ullens Center for Contemporary Art in Beijing's Art Factory 798.

SHELLEY WING CHAN, an associate professor of Chinese language and cultural studies at Wittenberg University, teaches courses in Chinese language, literature, and culture. A graduate of Hong Kong Baptist University, she earned her MA in East Asian languages and literature at the University of Wisconsin, Madison, and her PhD in comparative literature and humanities at the University of Colorado, Boulder. She previously taught at Stanford, the University of Colorado, Boulder, Beloit College, and Kalamazoo College. She has also done research on Tang poetry and popular literature of the Ming dynasty and written about gender issues from a cross-cultural perspective. Her book, entitled *A Subversive Voice in China*, on the fiction of Mo Yan, one of the most prominent contemporary writers in mainland China, was published in 2011, and she is editor of a volume of Mo Yan's selected stories for a Hong Kong publisher.

JULIE CHIU studied English language and literature and trotted a winding career path in and out of education. She then discovered the beauty of modern Chinese poetry at the City University of Hong Kong, where she earned her doctoral degree. As a teacher, she has worked with schoolkids, working adults, police officers, student teachers, and undergraduates. She is now happily engaged in the development of a core-text program at the Chinese University of Hong Kong that brings together Homer, Confucius, and Marx. She has published three books of translation, re-creating poetry, fiction, and history in a different tongue. Her scholarly writings cover such topics as tense and translation, the meter of Zheng Chouyu's poetry, translating Xiao Hong and Harry Potter, issues in Mahayana Buddhism, death and the tarot, and the happiness of a tree.

HOWARD Y.F. CHOY, an associate professor at Wittenberg University, received his PhD (Poetic heart Damage) in comparative literature and humanities from the University of Colorado. A journalist and theater critic from Hong Kong, he is interested in a comparative study of political jokes across mainland China, Hong Kong, Taiwan, and the US. Currently editing a book of Liu Zaifu's selected essays, he is the author of *Remapping the Past: Fictions of History in Deng's China, 1979–1997*. He has also published a number of articles and translations in major scholarly journals, including *positions, American Journal of Chinese Studies,* and *Asian Theatre Journal*.

CHI YU CHU studied English at the Tianjin Foreign Languages Institute and earned his PhD in comparative literature from the University of Hong Kong. He was assistant editor of *Renditions,* a magazine of English translations of Chinese literature, before joining the Polytechnic University, where he is now teaching translation studies. His publications include English translations of *A Chinese Winter's Tale* and *Selected Poems of Gu Cheng*.

JOHN A. CRESPI is the Henry R. Luce Associate Professor of Chinese at Colgate University in Hamilton, New York. His main area of research, modern and contemporary Chinese poetry, satisfies his desire to read and explain things he doesn't really understand, while leading many new acquaintances to expect that he writes poetry himself. Fortunately, he does not. His additional interests range from old Shanghai comic books and the entire city of Beijing to guitar, harmonica, native Upstate New York plants, rustic fencing, fishing, and any other constructive pursuit that does not seem like work.

JENNIFER FEELEY is an assistant professor of modern Chinese literature and culture at the University of Iowa, where she teaches courses in literature, cinema, and popular culture. She is currently writing a book on the impact of American confessional poetry on women's poetry in 1980s China. Her translations of contemporary Chinese poetry can be found in various books and journals.

HAOWEN GE is a freelance translator and former academic.

JI HAO was born in China. He got his bachelor's degree in Chinese literature from Renmin University. In 2004, he came to the US to pursue graduate study. In 2006, he obtained his MA from the University of Southern California. Currently a PhD student at the University of Minnesota, he is working on the hermeneutics of Du Fu's poetry. He has published articles on Chinese poetry and its English translation.

NICKY HARMAN lives in the UK and works as a freelance translator as well as teaching a translation studies course at Imperial College London. Her great passion is the translation of contemporary Chinese literature, and she has enjoyed working on many different kinds of writing within that broad category: novels, short stories, nonfiction, and—most recently—poetry. She loved translating these poems by Han Dong, because of their outward simplicity that conceals beneath the surface many layers of meaning and imagery.

MICHAEL GIBBS HILL is an assistant professor in the Department of Languages, Literatures, and Cultures at the University of South Carolina. He dedicates his translations in this collection to his first teacher of Chinese, Professor Kathleen Tomlonovic of Western Washington University.

YIBING HUANG was born in Changde, Hunan, China, and inherited Tujia ethnic minority blood from his mother. After receiving his BA, MA, and PhD in Chinese literature from Peking University, he moved to the US in 1993. He holds a second PhD in comparative literature from the University of California, Los Angeles. Under the pen name Mai Mang,

Huang has published poetry in China since the 1980s, and he recently has begun to translate his own poems into English. He is the author of two collections of poetry: *Stone Turtle: Poems 1987–2000* and *Approaching Blindness*. He is also the author of *Contemporary Chinese Literature: From the Cultural Revolution to the Future*, a book that presents case studies of the generation of Chinese writers who lived their formative years during the Cultural Revolution and focuses on their identity shift from "orphans of history" to "cultural bastards." Huang is currently an associate professor of Chinese at Connecticut College.

HEATHER INWOOD spent her childhood years in rural Cambridgeshire dreaming of becoming an international secret agent, before putting those plans on hold to study the flute at secondary school, then Chinese at Cambridge University. Armed with a PhD from the School of Oriental and African Studies (SOAS) in London, and a few years spent studying literature and involving herself in the media in China, she crossed the Atlantic to the US in 2008. She now works as assistant professor of modern Chinese cultural studies at The Ohio State University, where she teaches and researches contemporary Chinese poetry, pop culture, and media. Her first book is about the post-2000 mainland Chinese poetry scene.

NICK KALDIS is Director of Chinese Studies and an associate professor of Chinese studies in the Department of Asian and Asian-American Studies at Binghamton University (SUNY). He received his BA in English from Ohio University, an MA in English from Purdue University, and an MA and PhD in East Asian languages and literatures from The Ohio State University. He serves on the editorial boards of *Journal of Chinese Cinemas* and *Modern Chinese Literature & Culture*, and is literature book review editor for the latter. His teaching and scholarship focus on Chinese cinema, literature, and language. He has published essays on modern Chinese literature and contemporary Chinese film, as well as numerous translations. His current projects include a book-length study of Lu Xun's *Yecao* and a co-edited collection of nature-writing essay translations from the works of Liu Kexiang.

RONALD M. KIMMONS is a graduate of Brigham Young University with degrees in English and Chinese. Some of his favorite things in the world are his hot wife, Alcione, egregiously expensive electric sports cars, nerdy board games, metaphysical poetry, and grunge rock. He believes in Jesus, dreams of developing telekinetic powers, and hates having animals in the house.

RICHARD KING is at the University of Victoria in Canada, where he teaches Chinese language, literature, and popular culture and academic methodology. His research is on modern and contemporary literature, cultural history, and popular culture, and he has translated the work of a number of contemporary authors. Recent publications are *Art in Turmoil*, an edited volume on the arts of the Cultural Revolution, and *Heroes of China's Great Leap Forward*, translations of two works of fiction from 1960 and 1980.

LUCAS KLEIN is a writer, translator, and editor of CipherJournal.com. His translations, essays, and poems have appeared or are forthcoming at *Two Lines, Chinese Literature Today, Jacket*, and *Drunken Boat*, and he regularly reviews books in *Rain Taxi* and elsewhere. Now an assistant professor in the Department of Chinese, Translation, and Linguistics at City University of Hong Kong, he is working on translations of Tang dynasty poet Li Shangyin, in addition to contemporary poet Xi Chuan.

CHARLES A. LAUGHLIN has a BA in Chinese language and literature from the University of Minnesota, a master of arts, master of philosophy, and PhD in Chinese literature from Columbia University, and is currently Weedon Chair Professor of East Asian Studies at the University of Virginia. He has published extensively on Chinese literature from the 1920s to the 1960s, including two books: *Chinese Reportage: The Aesthetics of Historical Experience* and *The Literature of Leisure and Chinese Modernity*. Laughlin also has been translating contemporary Chinese poetry for over fifteen years. His current research is on discourses of desire in Chinese revolutionary literature.

MABEL LEE, PhD, Fellow of the Australian Academy of the Humanities (FAHA), is an adjunct professor of Chinese studies at the University of Sydney. Her area of research is modern and contemporary Chinese writers and writings, and she has published on Zhang Taiyan, Liang Qichao, Lu Xun, Liu Zaifu, Yang Lian, and Gao Xingjian. Her translation of Gao Xingjian's novel *Soul Mountain* brought her international recognition when Gao was declared 2000 Nobel Laureate for Literature. She translated Gao's second novel, *One Man's Bible,* a collection of his short stories, *Buying a Fishing Rod for My Grandfather,* and his book of critical essays, *The Case for Literature.* She also translated three collections of poetry by Yang Lian, 1999 winner of the International Flaiano Prize for Poetry. Yang's *Masks and Crocodile* and *The Dead in Exile* were published in 1990, and his long poem inspired by the *Yijing* (*The Book of Changes*), entitled *Yi,* was published in 2002.

ANDREA LINGENFELTER is a poet, scholar, and translator of Chinese, and 2008 recipient of a PEN Translation Fund Grant. Her published translations include *The Changing Room,* a collection of poems by China's foremost feminist poet, Zhai Yongming, as well as the novels *Farewell My Concubine,* by Lilian Lee, and *Candy,* by Mian Mian. Her translations of contemporary poetry from mainland China, Taiwan, and Hong Kong have appeared in many anthologies and journals, including *Frontier Taiwan, Zoland Poetry, The Literary Review, Hayden's Ferry Review,* and *Full Tilt.* Her prose translations have been published in *Kyoto Journal, Foreign Policy,* and *Chinese Writers on Writing.*

ALICE XIN LIU was born in Beijing and left for London at the age of seven, returning when she was twenty-one. In that time, she'd had the good fortune of studying English literature at Durham University, UK, and being taught traditional Chinese language and culture every summer by Communist cadre grandparents. Now, Liu is still an enthusiastic reader of Chinese, Japanese, and English fiction and poetry. Since translation was part of her consciousness at a very young age, it's hard to see an alternative path. This is her first experience of translating poetry, but the feel has nevertheless lit an intense appreciation. In 2011 she finished a translation of a book of Shen Congwen's letters for a publishing house in China.

CHRISTOPHER LUPKE (PhD, Cornell University) is associate professor of Chinese and Coordinator of Asian Languages at Washington State University. He concurrently serves as the president of the Association for Chinese and Comparative Literature. Lupke has published two books as editor—*The Magnitude of Ming: Command, Allotment, and Fate in Chinese Culture* and *New Perspectives on Contemporary Chinese Poetry*—as well as numerous articles and book chapters. His forthcoming book is *Hou Hsiao-hsien*. He also has completed translations of Peng Ge's novel *Setting Moon* and Ye Shitao's *A History of Taiwan Literature*.

GERALD MAA is a co-editor of *The Asian American Literary Review*. His translations of Hai Zi have appeared in places such as *Chinese Writers on Writing, Circumference, Poetry Northwest,* and *Common Knowledge*, earning him a Florence Tan Moeson Fellowship from the Library of Congress Asian Reading Room as well as a translation grant from the International Center for Writing and Translation. He has also received scholarships to the Bread Loaf conference and has work in *American Poetry Review* and *Studies in Romanticism*. Having earned an MFA from the University of Maryland, Gerald is currently a PhD student in the English department at the University of California, Irvine.

PAUL MANFREDI is an associate professor of Chinese and chair of the Chinese Studies Program at Pacific Lutheran University. His research concerns modern and contemporary Chinese poetry and art, modernism, and urban culture in China. His articles have appeared in *Modern Chinese Literature and Culture, Journal of Modern Literature in Chinese, Yishu: Journal of Contemporary Chinese Art,* and *World Art*, while his translations have appeared in the journal *Mānoa* as well as in collections of modern and contemporary Chinese poetry. He has recently moved with his family to Bellevue, Washington, a small city that is slowly but surely surpassing its status as mere "Seattle suburb."

MARTIN MERZ grew up in Australia where he earned a BA (honors) in Chinese language and literature from Melbourne University before heading to Asia. After running around China for two decades doing China trade, Martin took an MA in applied translation from the Open University of Hong Kong. He co-translated Wang Gang's novel *English* in 2009 with Jane Weizhen Pan. Martin is still running around China doing China trade.

THOMAS MORAN lives in Ripton, Vermont, and is a professor of Chinese at Middlebury College. He has published translations of Chinese short stories and plays, and he is the editor of *Dictionary of Literary Biography*

Volume 328: Chinese Fiction Writers, 1900–1949. His current research interest is the writing of nature in modern and contemporary China.

JONATHAN S. NOBLE works with the University of Notre Dame's Provost Office on Asia Initiatives. He received a PhD in East Asian languages and literatures from The Ohio State University in 2003. Noble's research focuses on contemporary Chinese cultural studies. He has translated film scripts for over thirty Chinese films, including Li Yang's *Blind Shaft*, winner of the 2002 Silver Bear at the Berlin Film Festival, and Feng Xiaogang's blockbusters *Assembly* and *Aftershock*. Noble translated three Chinese plays—Huang Jisu, Zhang Guangtian, and Shen Lin's *Che Guevara*, Ouyang Yuqian's *After Returning Home*, and Tian Han's *The Night the Tiger Was Caught*—for *The Columbia Anthology of Modern Chinese Drama*. He started scribbling poetry during AP calculus classes at George C. Marshall High School after having read Ralph Waldo Emerson's "Brahma."

GEORGE O'CONNELL is a former Fulbright Professor of Creative Writing and American Literature at Peking University, and has taught creative writing and literature at numerous colleges and universities in the US and China. Among his honors are *Atlanta Review*'s International Grand Prize for Poetry, *Nimrod International Journal*'s Pablo Neruda Award, *Bellingham Review*'s 49th Parallel Prize, *Marlboro Review*'s Award in Poetry, and the 2007 China Journey Award. With Diana Shi, he co-edited/co-translated the 2008 *Atlanta Review* China Issue. Currently he and Ms. Shi are gathering and translating contemporary Chinese poetry for their own anthology, to be published in the US.

MIKE O'CONNOR is a poet who has authored four books of poetry and four books of translation from the Chinese, including *When I Find You Again, It Will Be in Mountains: Selected Poems of Chia Tao (779–842)* and *Where the World Does Not Follow: Buddhist China in Picture and Poem*. An NEA Fellow for translation and a Washington State Artist Trust Fellow for poetry, O'Connor was a small-scale farmer and woods worker before pursuing a career as a journalist in Taiwan for fifteen years. He currently lives in Port Townsend, Washington, and caretakes forest land on the Big Quilcene River. In 2010, he published *Immortality*, a book of original poetry.

JANE WEIZHEN PAN grew up in China's far north and moved to southern China at the age of eleven. She holds an MA in translation studies from Monash University and co-translated Wang Gang's novel *English* with Martin Merz. Jane is an interpreter of Mandarin, Cantonese, and English and taught graduate-level translation and interpreting at RMIT University in Melbourne. She is now pursuing a PhD at the Australian National University, researching nonsense literature in translation, with special emphasis on the strange life of *Alice in Wonderland* in China.

STEVE RIEP heads the Chinese section and teaches modern and contemporary Chinese literature, film, and culture at Brigham Young University. A California native, he received his BA in Chinese and political economy from the University of California, Berkeley, and his PhD from the University of California, Los Angeles in modern and contemporary Chinese literature. He has translated modern and contemporary Chinese poetry, fiction, drama, and essays. His research interests include the depiction of visual disabilities in transnational Chinese cinema, literary and filmic responses to Nationalist propagandistic street-naming policies in Taipei from the late-1940s to the 1990s, and the use of detective-fiction narrative techniques to recover the White Terror in fiction and film from Taiwan. His long-term book projects focus on literature and visual culture in Nationalist-era Taiwan (1949–1999) and disabilities in transnational Chinese cinema and literature.

TZE-LAN D. SANG is associate professor of Chinese literature at the University of Oregon. She has written on a wide range of topics in modern Chinese literature and culture. Among her major publications is *The Emerging Lesbian: Female Same-Sex Desire in Modern China*, a study of the formation of new sexual identities and disciplines of the self in twentieth-century China. She is currently working on two major projects, one on early twentieth-century Chinese popular fiction, the other on Taiwanese documentary films. She has published original Chinese short fiction previously and has translated Chinese short stories and poems into English.

DIANA SHI is a native Mandarin speaker and literary translator whose work has appeared in international literary journals such as *Circumference*, *Words without Borders*, and an anthology titled *The Frontier Tide*. She co-translated the recent film *Crossing the Mountain*, and co-edited/co-translated the 2008 *Atlanta Review* China Issue. She and George O'Connell are gathering and translating contemporary Chinese poetry for their own anthology, to be published in the US.

JONATHAN STALLING is an assistant professor of English literature at the University of Oklahoma specializing in transpacific poetry and poetics and is the co-founder and deputy editor-in-chief of *Chinese Literature Today*. Stalling is the author of *Poetics of Emptiness, Grotto Heaven,* and the forthcoming books *Yíngēlìshī (Chanted Songs, Beautiful Poetry): Sinophonic English Poetry and Poetics* and *Winter Sun: The Poetry of Shi Zhi 1966–2007*. He lives in Norman, Oklahoma, with his wife and children.

KUO-CH'ING TU, born in Taichung, Taiwan, graduated from National Taiwan University in 1963 with a major in English literature and received his MA in Japanese literature from Kwansei Gakuin University in 1970 and his PhD in Chinese literature from Stanford University in 1974. His research interests include Chinese literature, Chinese poetics and literary theories, comparative literature East and West, and worldwide literatures in Chinese. He is the author of numerous books of poetry in Chinese, as well as a translator of English, Japanese, and French works into Chinese and of contemporary Chinese works into English. He is a professor of Chinese in the Department of East Asian Languages and Cultural Studies at the University of California, Santa Barbara, and co-editor of *Taiwan Literature: English Translation Series*.

LISA LAI-MING WONG is an associate professor in humanities at the Hong Kong University of Science and Technology. She is the author of *Rays of the Searching Sun: The Transcultural Poetics of Yang Mu*. Her publications on modern Chinese poetry and Chinese-Western literary relations have appeared in journals such as *New Literary History, The Comparatist, The Keats and Shelley Review* (UK), *Canadian Review of Comparative Literature,* and *Modern China*. To her, poetry translation is a pleasure and a creative way to foster intercultural understanding.

MICHELLE YEH received her BA from National Taiwan University and her PhD from the University of Southern California. She is a professor at the University of California, Davis, where she teaches all genres of traditional and modern Chinese literature. Her recent publications include *Essays on Modern Poetry from Taiwan, A Lifetime Is a Promise to Keep: Poems of Huang Xiang,* and chapter 7 of *Cambridge History of Chinese Literature*.

TERRY SIU-HAN YIP is a professor in the Department of English Language and Literature at Hong Kong Baptist University. She received her MA and PhD from the University of Illinois, Urbana-Champaign, and has been teaching at HKBU since 1985. Her publications and translations can be found in anthologies, academic books, and journals published in Australia, Canada, China, Europe, India, Japan, Hong Kong, Taiwan, and the US.

TRANSLATORS' NOTES

53 "One day"
My road and *my terrace* refer to a stone stairway the poet built up a hill and a wooden balcony he nailed together.

75 "Exploring the Tomb of the First Emperor"
The poem contemplates the as-yet unopened tomb of the First Emperor of the Qin dynasty (259–210 BCE), the man who first united the six major states into the first Chinese dynasty, and constructed the earliest portions of the Great Wall. The Emperor's tomb complex near modern-day Xi'an, which includes the famous army of terra-cotta soldiers, is one of the largest in human history.

   The poem refers to many related figures and lore. Gongsun Long (325–250 BCE) was a famous logician of the previous Warring States Period; his paradoxical dialogues "On Hard or White" and "On 'White Horse'" continue to confound scholars. Li Si (280–208 BCE) was a famous Legalist philosopher who served as the First Emperor's prime minister, whose accomplishments include the standardization of weights and measures and the Chinese writing system. But his draconian legal code also was highly intolerant of intellectual diversity and resulted in the burning of all heterodox books and the persecution of Confucians and proponents of other philosophies. Xu Fu (255–210? BCE) was the First Emperor's court sorcerer who, near the end of the Emperor's life, was sent on an expedition to the Eastern Seas to retrieve the elixir of immortality, a journey from which he never returned. In 212 the Emperor built the enormous Epang Palace, which was burned to the ground shortly after the dynasty's end.

91 "Bringing Home a New Book about Six Dynasties Literati"
Ji Kang (223–262) was a poet, musician, and Taoist in the Wei dynasty, and a leader of the group of literary figures known as the Seven Sages of the Bamboo Grove (*zhulin qixian*). He married into a powerful political family but incurred the displeasure of the Sima family, who controlled the dynasty, and was executed. Zuo Si (250–305) was a poet of the Western Jin dynasty. He wrote a series of poems on history, one of which is about the assassin Jing Ke (d. 227 BCE). Remembered and admired for his bravery, Jing Ke was killed during his failed attempt to assassinate Ying Zheng (who later became the first emperor of China, Qin Shihuang). Both Ji Kang and Zuo Si promoted a retreat to the countryside as a refuge from the dangerous politics at the imperial court.

111 "Burned-Out Bulbs"
Sen Zi alludes to Plato's *Republic* (ca. 380 BCE).

115 "Staying Overnight on a Mountain"
"The starry sky…" is from Kant's *Critique of Practical Reason* (1788).

187 "Unfinished Journey"
Shihuang de ren, literally "men who glean or collect scraps," refers here to migrants from the countryside who use whatever skills they have to eke out subsistence in the city.

 Wormwood (artemisia) is a plant associated with Dragon Boat Festival, a festival memorializing China's first great poet, Qu Yuan. Leaves of the plant, placed in windows and on doorsills, are said to ward off contagious diseases and evil spirits.

197 "1967"
The *erhu* is a widely used two-stringed instrument played with a bow. The *qin*, with seven strings, resembles a long, narrow zither.

209 "The Previous Life"
This poem alludes to the Chinese legend of "The Butterfly Lovers," Liang Shanbo and Zhu Yingtai. "The Previous Life" probably refers to their tragic love story in human society before they are united after death in the world of butterflies.

213 "The Night Revels of Han Xizai, a Handscroll"
There are two other versions of Han Xizai's story. One has it that Emperor Li suspected that Han might rebel against him. In the other version the emperor offered to make Han his prime minister; the offer was rejected, leaving the emperor curious as to why. Both versions may explain why Han looks pensive, almost melancholy amid the revelry in all five scenes depicted in the handscroll—he was either aware of his risky situation or he was sick of the dog's race in the court. Either way, he found escape in embracing or faking sensual indulgence. When unrolled, from right to left, the horizontal handscroll depicts five scenes: the pipa song, the dance, the repose, the flute concerto, and the farewell. It enables the viewer to stop and focus on any scene or frame and move at any pace. This allows volatile, multiple perspectives rather than a fixed, single perspective, as in Western painting.

243 "A Poem of a Wandering Immortal"
The Chinese tradition of abstruse poems about journeys made by shamans and Taoists through the world, the heavens, and the imagination goes back to the third century BCE and the poem "Lisao" ("Encountering Sorrows"). Guo Jingchun (Guo Pu, 276–324), for one, is known for "Poems of Wandering Immortals" (*youxianshi*), which also names a genre and is the title of Jiang Hao's poem. In Jiang Hao's case the immortal is the author, who has wandered to Ürümqi, Xinjiang, where he worked for a newspaper.

Its passing: Jiang Hao uses a phrase from Buddhism that refers to monks who pass away while sitting in meditation.

Magpie Bridge: In the legend of the Weaving Maid and the Herdboy, magpies join wing to wing to bridge the Milky Way so the separated lovers can meet.

Half the land is a set phrase that often connotes the unoccupied part of an invaded country.

Clouds and rain is a euphemism for sex.

Mutually restricting, mutually enhancing are terms from Yin-Yang and Five Elements doctrines.

Present in a single thought: Jiang Hao uses the phrase *yi nian san qian* ("the three thousand realms of existence present in a single thought-moment"), a notion developed in Tiantai Buddhism.

At your bliss: Jiang Hao uses a phrase, *sui xi,* that is associated with Buddhism and can mean "follow the good influence of a charitable person" or "visit a temple"; it also has the prosaic meaning of "do as you like."

A white horse is not a horse is an argument—or paradox, or language game— put forth in a famous essay by Gongsun Long around 300 BCE.

How goes the night? is the first line of the poem "Ting liao" (Torches blazing in the courtyard) in the ca. 600 BCE *Classic of Poetry (Shijing).*

Watch the sun come and go. Jiang Hao here alludes to the Han dynasty *yuefu* (rhapsody) "Ri chu ru" (The sun comes and goes) and the Li Bai poem "Ri chu ru xing" (Song of the coming and going of the sun).

269 "Village History"
Zeng Guofan (1811–1872), a native of Xiangxiang, Hunan, was a Confucian scholar, government official, and military general best known for raising the Xiang, or Hunan, Army that helped defeat the Taiping rebels in 1864.

Since 1972, Copper Canyon Press has fostered the work of emerging, established, and world-renowned poets for an expanding audience. The Press thrives with the generous patronage of readers, writers, booksellers, librarians, teachers, students, and funders—everyone who shares the belief that poetry is vital to language and living.

This project was made possible by an award from the

NATIONAL ENDOWMENT FOR THE ARTS.

MAJOR SUPPORT HAS BEEN PROVIDED BY:

THE **PAUL G. ALLEN** FAMILY *foundation*

golden lasso

Lannan

NATIONAL ENDOWMENT FOR THE ARTS

 WASHINGTON STATE ARTS COMMISSION

The Paul G. Allen Family Foundation

Amazon.com

Anonymous

Diana and Jay Broze

Beroz Ferrell & The Point, LLC

Golden Lasso, LLC

Gull Industries, Inc.
on behalf of William and Ruth True

Lannan Foundation

Rhoady and Jeanne Marie Lee

National Endowment for the Arts

Cynthia Lovelace Sears and Frank Buxton

Washington State Arts Commission

Charles and Barbara Wright

To learn more about underwriting
Copper Canyon Press titles, please call
360-385-4925 x103

The Chinese character for poetry is made up of two parts: "word" and "temple." It also serves as pressmark for Copper Canyon Press.

The English text is set in Fedra Serif, a contemporary typeface designed by Peter Biľak. Headings are set in Mendoza, a typeface designed by José Mendoza y Almeida. Book design and composition by Valerie Brewster, Scribe Typography. Chinese composition by Linguaset. Printed on archival-quality paper at McNaughton & Gunn, Inc.